_____ *A Travel History* _____
OF
MARTHA'S VINEYARD

A Travel History
OF
MARTHA'S VINEYARD

From Canoes and Horses to Steamships and Trolleys

THOMAS DRESSER

Foreword by Herbert Foster

THE
History
PRESS

Published by The History Press
Charleston, SC
www.historypress.com

Front cover, top left: Horsecar trolley in the campground, 1873. *Courtesy of Martha's Vineyard Antique Photos, Charlie Kernick*; *middle:* Dukes County Garage by Five Corners. *Courtesy of history.vineyard.net/photos, Chris Baer*; *right*: Active leaving Oak Bluffs pier. *Courtesy of Martha's Vineyard Antique Photos, Charlie Kernick*; *bottom*: Steamship *Naushon*, grounded in Vineyard Haven Harbor. *Courtesy of history.vineyard.net/photos, Chris Baer.*
Back cover, top: 1928 Model A Ford, refurbished by Will deBettencourt of Binks. *Courtesy of Joyce Dresser*; *inset*: *Nobska* weather vane in Oak Bluffs. *Courtesy of Joyce Dresser.*

First published 2019

Manufactured in the United States

ISBN 9781467140003

Library of Congress Control Number: 2019932633

Notice: The information in this book is true and complete to the best of our knowledge. It is offered without guarantee on the part of the author or The History Press. The author and The History Press disclaim all liability in connection with the use of this book.

This book is dedicated to our grandchildren:
Lassi and Pinja in Helsinki, Finland; Vivienne and August in New Orleans,
Louisiana; Shealyn and Jocelyn in Edgartown, Massachusetts;
and Molly, Dylan and Henry in Los Angeles, California.

CONTENTS

Foreword, by Herbert L. Foster   9

Prologue   11

Acknowledgements   13

1. Early Transport to the Vineyard: 1600–1800   15
2. Early Steamships: 1830–1900   21
3. Dr. Fisher Road: 1858–1886   29
4. Steamship Service Comes of Age: 1860–1900   39
5. Horse-Drawn Trolley Cars: 1873–1895   47
6. The Era of the Electric Trolley Car: 1895–1917   53
7. The Martha's Vineyard Railroad: 1874–1895   63
8. Getting Around Vineyard Waters in the Early Twentieth Century   87
9. Early Automobiles on Martha's Vineyard: 1900–1930   93
10. Ferry Service: 1900–1924   105
11. Airplanes on the Vineyard: 1919–1940   109
12. Steamships: 1925–1950   115
13. Buses, Trucks and Tour Buses: 1920–Present   127
14. Steamship Travel: 1950–Present   135
15. Getting to the Vineyard in the Twenty-First Century   143

Epilogue   147
Notes   149
Bibliography   155
Index   157
About the Author   159

FOREWORD

When I took my army basic training in Camp Crowder in Joplin, Missouri, at the end of World War II, drummed into our eighteen-year-old heads was the expression "It depends on the terrain and situation." That dictum is very much related to Thomas Dresser's book on the history of traveling on Martha's Vineyard. Indeed, you can't write about transportation without mentioning the roads over which people, oxen, horses, bicycles and eventually cars and trucks made their way.

When I was a little guy and our country was in the middle of the Great Depression, my mother would take my two brothers and me from Brooklyn to a working farm in Richfield Springs, New York. Outside the village in the farmlands, roads were being built with a process of putting down tar and stone chips. Hot liquid tar would be sprayed on a gravel surface, and clean, small, dry stone chips would be distributed onto the hot liquid tar. The cooling tar would bring together the stone chips, forming the road. Interestingly, this road-building technique was used for building most roads in the United States prior to the 1930s. While the tar cooled and became a road, tar was on your shoes and everywhere—one of the negatives about road building in those days.

Thanks to Tom, we can read about the history of "getting" to Martha's Vineyard and getting around once here. Since we are an island, Tom helps us think about numbers of people getting here via steamships, smaller groups getting here by boat and finally people flying here. Of course, once here, figuring out how to get around was a challenge.

Herbert Foster.

As the number of "wash-ashore" Vineyard residents increases, Tom's book becomes more meaningful as he reports on his research related to transportation on our island. In the 1930s, the New England Steamship Company provided ferry service to the Vineyard. The passenger fare was one dollar and took two hours. Coming over with a car would set you back five to eight dollars.

According to Tom, we had horse and electric trolleys here. There was even a railroad to take visitors from Oak Bluffs to an ocean-side hotel in Edgartown. There was the Dr. Fisher Road to take one up-island. Early planes landed at the Katama grass airport. Our present main airport is here thanks to the 1943 World War II building of a naval air station. Seaplanes landed in the water on calm days and pulled up close to shore. Many years ago, I sailed to the Vineyard, and on that trip, we anchored in Lake Tashmoo. Just before falling asleep, we heard the roar of a seaplane landing and then taking off.

If you have an inquisitive mind and would like to become more knowledgeable about the history of travel on Martha's Vineyard and, in the process, become a Vineyard travel maven, then turn the page and get started on *A Travel History of Martha's Vineyard: From Canoes and Horses to Steamships and Trolleys.* Thomas Dresser's book is a must-read.

HERBERT L. FOSTER is an emeritus professor, Graduate School of Education, State University of New York at Buffalo, and author of *Ghetto to Ghetto: Yiddish and Jive in Everyday Life.*

PROLOGUE

When I first lived in Oak Bluff on Martha's Vineyard and worked in Falmouth, on the mainland, I commuted aboard the steamship *Islander* across Vineyard Sound for three years in the late 1990s. As a passenger on the steamship, my time was always a relaxing opportunity to read or write, to appreciate a few minutes of downtime, to savor the forced inactivity and personal time. Even today, I reflect wistfully on that quiet abode aboard the steamship, all to myself.

An amusing aspect of the ride is the recollection of the words of one purser, T.M. Araujo. Without fail, as we pulled into port, he alerted passengers it was time to prepare to debark. He would announce, "If you're on the right side, you're on the wrong side. Cross over to the left side to exit the boat." Twenty years later, those amusing words resonate whenever we approach port.

Darren Morris patiently trained me to drive a school bus and accompanied me when I earned my Commercial Driver's License over on the other side. A tense moment in the test was the approach to a railroad crossing. (Today, there are no railroad tracks on Martha's Vineyard.) I stopped the school bus, opened the door, checked the track both ways and proceeded across. Darren smiled, as did the licenser. I continued on the test and was returning to the beginning when we approached the railroad tracks again. I knew the licenser knew I knew what to do, so I thought I could proceed to the finish line without stopping at the track. Fortunately, at the last moment, I realized I had to stop; that was part of the test. I went through the drill and earned my CDL.

For nearly fifteen years, I drove a school bus across the hilly terrain of West Tisbury, picking up and dropping off high school students and a second run of elementary students. I met myriad students over the years and enjoyed the opportunity to become a small part of their lives for a brief time, then we both moved on.

In season, from May to October, I drove a tour bus for Scott Dario of Island Transport. For a couple of hours I was behind the wheel, driving fifty-five miles around the Island, at the microphone, glancing up at the mirror at my charges, captive or comatose to my historical anecdotes and hysterical humor. In tour bus driving, there is a lack of personal contact: no opportunity for give and take, question and response. Nevertheless, it was a fun run for a number of years.

Now I have relegated myself to auto tours, cruising around the Island whenever the opportunity arises and showing up in the annual July Fourth and Christmas parades in my bright-red 1948 Jeepster convertible—a perfect way to savor and share the role transportation continues to play across the Vineyard.

ACKNOWLEDGEMENTS

I t's easy to say that this book, or any book, is a compilation of suggestions and ideas, thoughts and concepts from a variety of people. Yet those people took the time and made the effort to make this book more comprehensive, readable, authentic and accurate. To all who lent a hand or a suggestion, my deepest thanks.

Sharon Kelley of Secret Garden suggested the topic. Cynthia Aguilar shared her research on West Tisbury byways, primarily the Dr. Fisher Road. David Foster added input. Bill Veno, James Lengyel and Adam Moore offered descriptive details.

Darren Morris provided valuable information on the Vineyard Transit Authority.

Karen Zingg shared specific details about the route of the Martha's Vineyard Railroad. Brendan O'Neill shared details of the Katama route.

Bridget Tobin provided background on steamship service between Woods Hole and the Vineyard. Mark Lovewell added tidbits to the story. Herb Ward shared the background of Captain Charles Leighton; great-granddaughter Erin Leighton added to the tale.

Will DeBettencourt offered time and information on his antique autos. Hilary Wall, the *Gazette* librarian, was a ready referral source on early automobiles on the Vineyard.

A host of research material covers various means of transport, from Arthur Railton's *Martha's Vineyard History* to a pair of books on the Martha's Vineyard Railroad, one by Herman Page and another by Walter Blackwell. Several steamship books supplemented articles in various periodicals.

Bow Van Riper of the Martha's Vineyard Museum offered immeasurable assistance in tracking down files of various modes of transport. I look forward to future research experience in the "new" Martha's Vineyard Museum in Vineyard Haven.

Photographs were generously provided by Chris Baer of history. vineyard.net and Charlie Kernick of Martha's Vineyard Antique Photos. Pictures add immeasurably to the finished product, and I am most grateful for their generosity.

Daniel Serpa, an Edgartown middle school student, participated in the research for this book. He used a metal detector to search his grandmother's backyard to uncover a railroad spike. An ancestor, Ebeneezer Earl (1856–1932), was the Edgartown jailer and, according to his obituary in the *Vineyard Gazette*, was "one of the few survivors of the old Martha's Vineyard Railroad on which he saw employment in many capacities." Also, Joseph Serpa, Daniel's great-grandfather, sold land to the Katama Airfield in 1946. Daniel's great-grandparents' house was converted into the Right Fork Diner.

My wife, Joyce, spent the time to take photographs, from Kennebunk's Seashore Trolley Museum to the train track route through Edgartown. Joyce has been an essential editor on this project, combing through the manuscript to capture and (hopefully) correct each error.

As a coda, I recognize the talents and knowledge of The History Press crew who waded through the images, challenged my grammatical shenanigans and prepared a finished product we can all be proud of. Thank you, Mike Kinsella and Hilary Parrish. Marketing maven Dani McGrath put on the final touch by promoting the book all across New England.

Chapter 1

EARLY TRANSPORT TO THE VINEYARD

1600–1800

N ative Americans have called Martha's Vineyard home for ten thousand years. The local tribe, the Wampanoag, lived in temporary settlements by the seashore in the warmer months, harvesting the bounties of ocean shellfish and freshwater fish in various streams. Drift whales washed up on the beach due to the change of tides, chased by predators or disease, providing a massive amount of ready meat.

Families or small groups of Native Americans were centered by the natural resources of their environment and moved easily and often around *Noepe*, as they called the Vineyard (*Noepe* translates to "amid the waters" in the Wopanaak language), as the seasons changed. In cooler weather, the Wampanoag closed up their *wetus* and carted them inland to more protected sites. There they gathered nuts, berries and leaves and found adequate hunting throughout the winter. "The movement of people within homelands [occurred] through the seasons as resources and conditions varied."[1]

Natives used fire sparingly, to cook and control their environment, making the landscape more conducive to hunting by burning the lower branches of trees. That made it easier to capture and kill small animals and hunt their primary target, white-tail deer. While the Wampanoag conducted burning to assist with agriculture and berry growth, they did not disturb their environment. Native fires caused no long-term ecological disruption to the landscape. However, "across the Vineyard and coast, fire appears to link the history of an ancient race and modern conservation."[2]

When Natives traveled across the Vineyard, they walked over a long, level landscape, along well-worn pathways on trails where animals first ran. One early trail ran parallel to Vineyard Sound mostly along the shore from Vineyard Haven harbor down to the southwest corner of the Island. Another trail ran east and west, just north of the inlets and ponds on the south shore, linking the eastern settlement of Nunnepog with Takemmy in the west, a forerunner of the Edgartown–West Tisbury Road. Native American trails crisscrossed the Vineyard more than on neighboring Nantucket because the Vineyard has a larger and more diverse landscape and was home to several separate sites of Wampanoag Native Americans.

Without horses, the twenty-mile route across the Island would have taken time. Horses did not appear as a means of Wampanoag transit prior to the arrival of the white man in the 1600s. Oxen arrived with the white settlers as well, and the Wampanoag found a ready use in their hilly Gay Head landscape. Oxen were slow but steady, good for tilling the ground but not for long treks to the northern and eastern settlements.

Native Americans explored their nautical environs as well, paddling their canoes through local harbors and across Vineyard Sound to the Cape. It is very likely Native Americans visited the nearby Elizabeth Islands and crossed Vineyard Sound to the mainland. The Island was close enough to the mainland that it could be reached by dugout canoe.

With minimal tools, a dugout was a tedious challenge to create. The largest Vineyard trees, oak and maple, were difficult to chop down, so Natives used a dead tree that had already fallen. They then had to burn out the core of the trunk. Dugouts were used when the Wampanoag interacted with mainland tribes.

Evidence of contact is found in artifacts uncovered on the Vineyard dating back at least eight thousand years. This archaeological record indicates trade with other Natives in Massachusetts, Maine, upstate New York and even Labrador. Yet the Wampanoag on the Vineyard were a localized tribe, fishing, hunting and farming on native soil.

The Wampanoag supplemented their agrarian diet by hunting in the heavily wooded forests across the Vineyard and taking full advantage of the sea around them. "On the coast and across the region, we see a continuity in lifestyle over thousands of years based on hunting, fishing, and collecting of terrestrial, freshwater, and marine resources."[3] The Wampanoag had no need to travel to the mainland; all their necessities were available right on the Vineyard.

Wampanoag tribal members paddle a dugout canoe in Vineyard Haven Harbor to welcome the Hawaiian raft *Hokulea* in 2016. *Photo by Thomas Dresser*.

Native Americans on the Vineyard lived in a forested land where they were very much part of their natural surroundings. Wampanoag considered themselves part of the land around them, with no intent to destroy their homeland. "Abruptly, and only a few hundred years ago, this pattern was broken by the arrival of the new culture introduced by the white man. The contrast, in the pace of change and face of the New England landscape, could not have been more dramatic."[4] The impact on the Native Americans must have been devastating and frightening, and yet they managed to accommodate the newcomers with a minimum of strife.

Martha's Vineyard was already known to European explorers prior to its "discovery" by Bartholomew Gosnold in 1602. Previous adventurers had met Native Americans and shared a rudimentary knowledge of English and trinkets as they traded furs. Gosnold was just another "discoverer," primarily in search of gold but curious about the lost colony of Roanoke. Gosnold's vessel, the *Concord*, was manned by a crew of thirty-two who harvested a ton of sassafras, the product of choice, on Cuttyhunk; it was then transported back to England. Sassafras root was brewed as a tea as an antidote for gout and syphilis.

The concept of "first contact" is a misnomer for the gradual interaction among numerous English, Dutch, French and Spanish explorers and various tribes of Native Americans that occurred over a long period. When we consider that Leif Eriksson landed on Newfoundland in the year 1000 and possibly the Vineyard around the same time, the era of interaction between Natives and the explorers is expansive.

Travel to America aboard the sailing vessels of the early seventeenth century was arduous. Journeys were ripe with potential disease and disaster from storms at sea. Nevertheless, more and more captains mounted expeditions to the New World. And Native Americans were taken aboard ship and exhibited in Europe. Squanto, who assisted the settlers at Plimoth Plantation, traveled across the Atlantic five times, and the Vineyarder Epinow was another transatlantic Wampanoag traveler.

Thomas Mayhew settled on the Vineyard, in Great Harbour (now Edgartown), in 1642. Sailing ships established transatlantic routes. The crossing would be measured in weeks or months, hardly at the whims or needs of the settlers. And disaster could easily disrupt transatlantic trips. Thomas Mayhew Jr., age thirty-nine, son of the founder, was lost at sea when his ship disappeared in 1657 en route to England for supplies needed by the new colony. This tragedy exemplified the dangers of ocean transit but did not hinder future seafarers from the call of the sea.

Once settlement on the Vineyard was underway shortly after Thomas Mayhew and his fellow settlers landed, primitive roadways were laid out in Great Harbour. Roadways often followed Native American trails. Scotchman's Bridge Road in West Tisbury was laid out in 1666.

From Edgartown, known to the Natives as Nunnepog, settlers tracked across the island to Takemmy, where an early mill was located by the Mill Pond. Today, this route is the Edgartown–West Tisbury Road. This was originally known as South Road, opened in 1738, which followed the Native American trail north of inlets along the south shore. A map as recent as 1956 labeled this Takemmy Road, describing the route to the mill in West Tisbury.

The Holmes Hole Road linked West Tisbury to Vineyard Haven in the north as early as 1670. The route was circuitous, from West Tisbury to

Middleton through Lambert's Cove, again following the original route of the Native Americans.

Another route to Holmes Hole was the Ferry Road from Edgartown to Vineyard Haven, where the boats left for Woods Hole. This route was first used in 1700, became a county road about 1850 and was dramatically transformed in the 1960s as the Vineyard's first federal highway.

One of the oldest Native American trails circumnavigated Gay Head village, including Toad Rock, a community meeting area or primitive post office. This route was dramatically redesigned and rebuilt in 1958 to provide ocean views to tour bus patrons. This is now known as Moshup Trail.

Once Martha's Vineyard hosted an established population, the need arose to establish a regular route to the mainland. Packets, small sailing ships that ran at the whim of the winds and their captains, transported passengers and goods across Vineyard Sound. By and large, these sloops, one mast with a sail and a jib, were the primary means of transit across Vineyard Sound well into the nineteenth century.

Scheduled sloops or packets sailed across Vineyard Sound along the shoreline, linking the coastal communities. Regularly scheduled sailings between Falmouth and Holmes Hole were in place early in the eighteenth century but always dependent on the wind. This type of sailboat made regular trips across the Sound but was neither a ferry nor organized as an established business.

One of several ports for packets was Lambert's Cove because it was closest to the mainland. Great Harbour, or Old Town, had a protected harbor and proved popular as it was the county seat and population center. Fishing sloops were a convenient means of transport but, again, subject to the captain's intent and the peculiarities of the weather.

Locally, a rowboat was put into service between Edgartown and Chappaquiddick once settlers developed a need to travel across Edgartown harbor to Chappaquiddick, which housed a Native American settlement. The Wopanaak word *Chappaquiddick* means "separated land," which defines the breach at Katama Bay that opens and closes with the vagaries of the ocean over the years.

Transport across the Vineyard was simple and direct in the days of Native Americans. Settlers brought new needs and demands to shape the landscape, though they often followed the route of Native Americans. As more people settled on the Vineyard and the local Wampanoag were decimated by disease, the necessity of reliable transport was influenced more directly by the current population.

Chapter 2

EARLY STEAMSHIPS

1830–1900

S ailing packets provided minimal service in linking the Vineyard with the mainland. The need was evident for a regular service between Martha's Vineyard, Nantucket and the mainland.

With Robert Fulton's invention of the steamboat in 1807, a more efficient means of transport was on the horizon.

Establishment of a regular service across the Sound proved a daring endeavor. It was not easy to establish a regular route to the mainland. The crew on the early packets required bravery and courage to ensure safe passage. Even today, the Steamship Authority acknowledges the risks and responsibilities of manning the route across Vineyard Sound.

"In July 1830, the *Marco Bozzaris*, carrying 210 passengers who were accompanied by the Bridgewater Band, traveled from New Bedford to Martha's Vineyard, making the first trip under steam into Edgartown Harbor."[5] This early side-wheeler, small and unwieldy, was the initial effort to link the Vineyard with the mainland. And why would a steamship bear the ungainly name of the *Marco Bozzaris* (1830–33)?

The origin of the name came from an employee in Jacob Barker's brokerage house. Barker was a Nantucket businessman involved in various enterprises, including the nascent steamship industry. Fitz-Greene

Halleck penned the following words, and his boss seized on the title for his new steamer:

> *"Marco Bozzaris"*
> *At midnight, in his guarded tent,*
> *The Turk was dreaming of the hour*
> *When Greece, her knee in suppliance bent,*
> *Should tremble at his power.*

The original Markos Botsaris was a general in the Greek war for independence from the Ottoman Empire in 1823. Botsaris died in the unsuccessful revolt.

> *Bozzaris! with the storied brave*
> *Greece nurtured in her glory's time,*
> *Rest thee: there is no prouder grave,*
> *Even in her own proud clime.*

Halleck became a popular poet in the mid-nineteenth century and an advisor for financier John Jacob Astor. The incongruous name of the steamship lives on as the first vessel to provide regularly scheduled steamship service between the Vineyard and the mainland—in this case, New Bedford.

The *Bozzaris* inaugurated service first to Nantucket in 1828, two years prior to the Vineyard service. On its initial run, Captain Edward Barker, nephew of the owner, ran the ship aground on rocks in New Bedford harbor. He was so embarrassed that he swore his crew and sole passenger to secrecy (a pact that apparently didn't stick).

Following the success of this first foray to Martha's Vineyard by the *Bozzaris*, in July 1830, a second steamship trip took place. "The following week she made a trip from Nantucket to the Vineyard with 150 Nantucketers, inaugurating the first excursion between the two islands. The fare was 75 cents, round trip, with entertainment being furnished by an 'orchestra' of three violinists."[6]

For three years, the *Bozzaris* steamed between Edgartown and New Bedford, occasionally operating excursions from the Vineyard to Nantucket or Hyannis. In the spring of 1832, the *Bozzaris* offered three regular trips a week, leaving Edgartown on Tuesdays, Thursdays and Saturdays and returning from New Bedford on Wednesdays, Fridays and Sundays.

Thus, the *Marco Bozzaris* inaugurated regularly scheduled steamship service to the Vineyard and ran successfully for three years. Aboard ship, the captain served as purser, collecting the two-dollar fare per passenger, as well as manning the helm of the vessel on the six-and-a-half-hour trip across Buzzards Bay from New Bedford to Edgartown.

While the *Marco Bozzaris* was the first steamship to link the islands of Martha's Vineyard and Nantucket to the mainland, it never proved a profitable venture. "There was little passenger travel in those days and the greater part of [the Vineyard and] Nantucket's commerce was carried on by means of sloops or 'packets,' which frequently made better time."[7] Nevertheless, it was an auspicious start for steamship service to the Vineyard, which grew in popularity and became more a necessity over the years.

Businessmen on the mainland recognized that steamships were an adequate means of transporting passengers and freight between the mainland and the Vineyard. Whilst some stalwarts bemoaned modern technological advances, the majority of the Vineyard populace sat back in a noncommittal mode to wait and see whether the steamboats were indeed a reliable means of transport.

Two years after the *Marco Bozzaris* steamed into Edgartown, the *Telegraph* (1832), weighing 171 tons, began operations between New Bedford and Nantucket, with a stop in Holmes Hole, as Vineyard Haven was then known.

During the winter, with the climate colder in the nineteenth century than it is now, harbor ice often hindered ferry service. Nantucket Harbor was frozen over many times, as were the harbors of the Vineyard.

The story goes that the *Telegraph* was a reliable icebreaker. For the vessel to plow through the ice fields, the captain would bark, "Everyone aft," and all the "passengers would be requested to 'go aft,' so that the steamer's bow, which was of very peculiar shape and had a tendency to ride on top of the ice instead of through it, could be run well up on the floe." Once the weight of the passengers congregating in the stern caused the bow of the ship to rise up onto the ice, the captain would call, "Everyone forward," and the passengers would dutifully dash to the bow and "by their weight assist the steamer in breaking through the ice."[8] Thus, the *Telegraph* passengers literally participated in crushing through the ice floes, hustling fore and aft as the ship slogged ponderously through the harbor.

During the ice-breaking activity, an engaging cabin boy played violin music on the deck to calm the passengers on their arduous journey.

Island residents gradually, grudgingly acknowledged the need for regularly scheduled service to the mainland and recognized that steamships consistently proved more reliable than sailboats. In response to this affirmation, a group of businessmen organized the Nantucket Steamboat Company in 1833 in expectation of the expanded demand for service to both islands.

A new steamship, the *Massachusetts* (1842), was put into service to supplement the *Telegraph*. The *Massachusetts* was a side-wheeler that cost $40,000. With two steamships working in tandem, passenger service improved dramatically, especially when the vessels added Edgartown to their route. Together, the *Telegraph* and the *Massachusetts* met the needs of the Vineyard and Nantucket. Still, many Vineyarders preferred sloops or packets, which sailed when they had sufficient business, in contrast to the regularly scheduled steamer service.

In November 1842, the steamship *Telegraph* left Nantucket bound for Edgartown, towing the whaling supply ship the *Joseph Starbuck*. "On board [the *Starbuck*] were a half dozen ladies, besides the members of the crew, the trip over to the Vineyard being a sort of pleasure cruise, which, however, resulted in disaster and loss of a splendid vessel."[9]

The *Starbuck* ran aground on the sandbar off Nantucket Harbor. The *Telegraph* was unable to haul it off and returned to Nantucket Harbor, leaving the passengers to ride out an approaching storm. During the night, the *Starbuck* capsized, and both passengers and crew faced danger and death. The next morning, the *Massachusetts* arrived and rescued everyone from the sinking ship. It was a dramatic example of the challenges and virtues of steamship service.

After that prominent rescue, the *Massachusetts* towed ships and conducted wrecking operations for the Nantucket Steamship Company, garnering additional income for the company. In 1854, an incident occurred when the *Massachusetts* itself ran aground off Mattapoisett while towing the Edgartown whaleship *Splendid* back to the Vineyard but managed to continue its journey and return the *Splendid* to Edgartown.

Another source of revenue for the Nantucket Steamship Company was generated by ownership and operation of the profitable Jared Coffin House. This continued for a decade, beginning in 1847. The Coffin House was a swank Nantucket hostelry that accommodated forty guests and a dozen horses.

With the prominence and profit generated by the whaling industry, Nantucket appeared at the apex of the economic ladder. However, the island was stymied by a sandbar off its harbor that prevented heavily laden whaleships from crossing the bar. In the mid-1840s, a Nantucket engineer developed a mechanical device that raised ships over the sandbar with pontoons filled with water that elevated the ships slightly. (This could have prevented the *Joseph Starbuck* from grounding.) For several years, this system of "camels" hoisted whaleships over the bar, but the process was deemed ineffective and discontinued in 1849.

An effort was made to improve service between Martha's Vineyard and New Bedford in 1845. A new ship, the *Naushon* (1845–48), was launched. The schedule was thrice-weekly runs between Edgartown and New Bedford, with occasional stops at Woods Hole and Holmes Hole. The *Naushon* was dedicated to serving the Vineyard.

An adventure for the *Naushon* was the first steamship trip to the cliffs of Gay Head on July 4, 1846. "In the afternoon, the steamer *Naushon* made an excursion to Gay Head, two hundred persons taking passage. Years later such excursions were to become famous."[10] Steamship passage could be an enjoyable experience, not just as a means to commute from one place to another.

Like many a predecessor, due to a dearth of passenger traffic, the *Naushon* failed financially and was closed down after only three years of operation. One reason for the demise of the *Naushon* was that the schedule, leaving Edgartown at 8:00 a.m., was deemed too early, especially for Vineyarders who lived up-Island, which necessitated a long, early morning ride by horse and buggy. Up-Islanders preferred to wait for the 10:00 a.m. *Massachusetts*, which docked in Holmes Hole. Passenger preferences were key to make service successful, even in the 1840s.

In 1851, the Martha's Vineyard Steamboat Company was formed, nearly twenty years after Nantucket had its own company. When the Nantucket Company considered abandoning New Bedford for Hyannis in 1854, the new venture re-formed as the New Bedford, Vineyard and Nantucket Steamboat Company and openly competed with the Nantucket Steamship Company for the incrementally increasing steamship passenger business.

Nantucketers were incensed that a rival company would move in on their territory. The *Vineyard Gazette* responded, "We would inform our Nantucket friends that this attempt of theirs to divide the Vineyard, especially the Edgartown travel, will not succeed. Their boat is not wanted here and will not be patronized." The *Gazette* predicted, "Our people know full well that the object of our Nantucket friends is to divide the travel, cause the withdrawal of the boat built expressly for our accommodation, and then leave us to whistle over deserted hopes."[11]

Today, a friendly rivalry exists between the two islands. The only antagonism that becomes physical and vocal occurs on the football field in the annual contest between the Vineyard and Nantucket high school teams.

The *Canonicus* (1851–61) was designed to handle the route from Fairhaven to Edgartown, beginning in 1851. (Canonicus was the name of the Narragansett chief who befriended the white settlers in Rhode Island.) Passenger doubts about another ferry curtailed ridership at first, but the *Canonicus* managed to stay in service for a decade. On occasion, the *Canonicus* ran excursions to Cottage City (now Oak Bluffs), fueling the Camp Meeting Association, until the onset of the Civil War, when it was requisitioned to serve in the Union navy.

When the *Canonicus* was withdrawn from passenger service, the schooner *John Oliver* met the needs of Vineyarders with sailing service between Edgartown and New Bedford. After the war, the *Canonicus* was used by a private firm, intermittently transporting religious revivalists from Providence, Rhode Island, to the Camp Meeting Association in Cottage City.

In 1854, the *Eagle's Wing* (1854–61) was launched, weighing 439 tons and 173 feet long. This was the first luxury steamer on Vineyard Sound, with a dining salon that accommodated eighty passengers. Word spread that the dining service was superb and a decent meal could be enjoyed for fifty cents while steaming across the Sound. The *Eagle's Wing* boasted two staterooms and fourteen berths. The vessel was "sumptuously decorated," even bearing a sign that read, "Ladie's Cabin," much to the annoyance of grammarians.

The *Eagle's Wing* operated primarily between Edgartown and New Bedford under Captain Benjamin Coffin Cromwell of Holmes Hole. Winters were rugged. During a particularly bleak spell in 1856, the *Eagle's Wing* was trapped in ice in Edgartown Harbor for nearly six weeks. And in Nantucket that winter, ice in the harbor was ten feet thick, eliminating any but the most hardy captain to brave the winter weather.

Over the years, the *Eagle's Wing* compiled a commendable resume until it succumbed to fire off Pawtuxet, Rhode Island, in 1861. The story goes that

Eagle's Wing was in an amicable race with another steamer, the *Perry* from Newport, until the *Eagle's Wing* caught fire. Fortunately, no one was injured. The steamship engine was salvaged and installed in a subsequent steamer, the *Monohansett*, which operated from 1865 to 1900.

"The new and beautiful steamer *Metacomet* (1854–56) which is to ply between this place and Fairhaven, arrived here on her first trip," proclaimed the *Vineyard Gazette* in 1854. Its arrival was greeted with great fanfare, cannon fire and "hearty cheers." (Metacomet, or King Philip, was the Wampanoag chieftain who led Native Americans in a rebellion against white settlers who had attacked the Wampanoag to take their land on the mainland in 1676. The decimation of the Wampanoag is described in Howard Zinn's *A People's History of the United States*: "When the English first settled Martha's Vineyard in 1642, the Wampanoags there numbered perhaps three thousand." By 1764, 122 years later, the population was only 313.)[12]

On occasion, the *Metacomet* visited Nantucket, once bringing Edgartown town officials and the Edgartown Quadrille Band in the summer of 1856. The next year, however, service was discontinued for financial reasons. The *Metacomet* served as a gunboat in the early years of the Civil War.

Another ship from this era, the *Island Home* (1855–96), was used primarily for the Nantucket run to New Bedford and later Hyannis, although it serviced the Vineyard occasionally over the years. The *Island Home* ran excursions from Nantucket to both the Vineyard and Hyannis in an effort to expand service and meet the needs of the various communities. At one time, the *Island Home* was considered the finest steamship to ply the waters off Cape Cod. The vessel was renovated extensively in 1887 and taken out of service in 1896 to be converted into a barge. The *Island Home* served the Islands for forty-one years, a record at the time. In 2007, a namesake vessel was introduced to the Vineyard, as high and imposing as an airport terminal—and fast. The *Island Home* zooms along at sixteen miles per hour and crosses the Sound in thirty-two minutes.

A short-lived vessel of this era was the propeller-driven steamboat the *Jersey Blue* (1856–57). The route of the *Jersey Blue* stretched from the East River in New York City to Edgartown, Holmes Hole and on to Nantucket. The *Jersey Blue* left New York every ten days, taking eight days to make the trek, with a day at each end to transfer freight. This ambitious enterprise only lasted a couple of years, but the concept was intriguing.

At the onset of the Civil War, the New Bedford, Vineyard and Nantucket Steamboat Company continued to operate the Edgartown and New Bedford route. Friction between the Nantucket and Vineyard steamship companies continued for the duration of the war. As one steamboat historian pointed out, "The trials and tribulations of these early steamboats had in the long run been very worthwhile. The stubborn island skepticism had given way by this time to general trust and admiration by the enterprising Yankees and paved the way for the next generation of steamboats."[13] Steamboats were here to stay.

Chapter 3

DR. FISHER ROAD

1858-1886

As residents of Martha's Vineyard were gradually accepting and adapting to the necessity and opportunity of steamship service to the mainland, they also recognized their need to travel across the Island itself. Transportation means were limited to horse and buggy, horseback or, up-Island, riding in ox carts. And when no other means of transport were available, there was always shank's mare, or walking. (The shank is the tibia or shinbone, essential to ambulation.)

The Vineyard is a landscape of nearly one hundred square miles, approximately twenty miles across and ten miles north to south. Various villages cropped up across the Island, quite isolated from one another. Ancient paths initially formed by deer and subsequently by the Wampanoag laced the island in an extensive network of trails. This web of rustic roadways, however, was not conducive to travel by wagon; horseback proved more efficient.

Enter Dr. Daniel Fisher, a wealthy entrepreneur who dominated nineteenth-century Martha's Vineyard. As an oil magnate, he became the wealthiest man on the Vineyard through his investments in the whaling industry. Fisher's business and political interests encompassed a huge swath of Vineyard life, from building a sidewalk in front of his house against the mud from North Water Street to the creation of the Martha's Vineyard National Bank, which survives to this day.

Fisher was born in Sharon, Massachusetts, in 1799. After undergraduate work at Brown University, he earned his medical degree at Harvard, followed by an internship at Massachusetts General Hospital. With that imposing résumé, he was invited to serve as a physician for sailors on Martha's Vineyard. Fisher gained additional credibility (and finances) when he married a local woman of a prominent Vineyard pedigree, Grace Cousens Coffin, in 1829 and opened his medical practice in town.

Not content to solely treat maritime mishaps, Fisher explored the opportunity to purchase whale oil and refine it; he then obtained the federal contract to sell it to lighthouse keepers along the coast. He stored thousands of barrels of oil at what became known colloquially as Fisher's Fort, now the Dukes County House of Correction. He established a spermaceti factory to produce candles from whale oil. He provided street lamps to illuminate downtown Edgartown, as long as the town purchased the necessary whale oil from him. Which it did.

And Dr. Fisher joined the baking business, establishing a hardtack bakery along the harbor by the present Old Sculpin Gallery. His intent was to bake hardtack and sell it to captains heading out on years-long whaling voyages. Hardtack is a firm, durable cracker or biscuit consisting of flour, salt and water. It lasts for a long time, making it feasible for captains to feed their crew on extensive whaling voyages.

"The great thing about hardtack is that as long as you keep it dry, it will last for years. It will even last through temperature extremes."[14] An authority on hardtack expands the rationale: "Because it's inexpensive to make and lasts so long, it was once taken on long sea voyages and was called things like pilot bread, cabin bread, ship biscuit, sea biscuit, or sea bread." Hardtack is best eaten when dipped in soup or coffee or broken up and fried. "It was particularly popular among soldiers during the American Civil War, and to this day Civil War re-enactors still make and carry hardtack with them."[15]

To bake his hardtack, Daniel Fisher needed flour. Rather than buy it, he bought farmland in West Tisbury, where he hired farmers to raise wheat and corn. His intent was to grow and grind his own grains then bake the hardtack. Dr. Fisher "acquired more than six hundred acres of land in West Tisbury to produce wheat raised by local farmers. Though this crop often faltered, with the slack filled by grain from Maryland, the *Gazette* carried ads for Fisher's flour into the 1870s, and the hardtack factory thrived until his death in 1876."[16] Fisher epitomized the nineteenth-century entrepreneur.

In 1858, Fisher built a mill, the Crocker Mill, on Crocker Pond off North Road by Seven Gates in what is now West Tisbury. (Dams along the Mill

Stream at the Fisher, now Woods, and Crocker Ponds are extant.) To ensure quality work at his mill, Fisher imported millstones from France and a miller from England.

Over the next two years, Dr. Fisher improved a ten-mile roadway from this mill to his bakery near Fisher's Pier on Dock Street in Edgartown, today the Old Sculpin Gallery. He created his road out of existing pathways. "Dr. Fisher chose a route north of the Mill Path (the straighter, more direct route between Edgartown and the West Tisbury Center) because it was less sandy and less hilly, also less populated as the soil was not good for farming." The description of the route continues: "Additionally, the small pond at the current State Forest Headquarters, Little Pond, near mid-point, served to water his horses."[17] (Little Pond has since dried up; it is a dry basin today.)

"Martha's Vineyard is crisscrossed with a network of ancient ways, most of which are far older than the Dr. Fisher Road. So parts of the route incorporated existing paths. Others were brand-new." Even as Dr. Fisher utilized paths already in use, he constructed a roadway that proved functional for his needs, avoiding populated areas and rugged terrain. "Dr. Fisher's Road passed through a relatively unpopulated area of the Island and by a pond that could supply water for the animals."[18]

"Fisher linked his two commercial centers across a singular ancient way that still bears his name. Dr. Fisher's Road is a delightful but occasionally obscure trail that arcs across the heart of the Great Plain from Edgartown to Middletown."[19] For nearly two decades, Fisher's eponymous roadway offered a faster, smoother route than the conventional old Mill Path with its numerous gates and bars, horse and wagon traffic and village activities to contend with.

Journeying north of the Mill Path meant Fisher's horse-drawn wagons did not have to struggle on the steep hills of the frost bottoms along the Mill Path and managed to make better time. The horse-drawn wagons were not slowed down by other wagons, the pasture bars or the busy village of West Tisbury. Until well into the 1870s, "the thriving enterprise of farms, mills, ponds, path, and factory advanced Dr. Fisher's local and global interest by feeding Vineyarders as they crisscrossed the seas."[20]

Ecologist David Foster added to his report on the Dr. Fisher Road: "The bulk of the road shows up clearly on Henry Whiting's [1850] map[21] and so it certainly was not created by Daniel Fisher expressly for his purposes." Foster continued. "It would be fascinating to learn of the earliest use of his name for it, but I'd suspect that his local importance and active use for some brief period just gave rise to the designation."[22]

"One can walk much of the route of Dr. Fisher's carriages with Island soil underfoot, through scenery that at least in parts must resemble how it looked in 1870." Tod Dimmick, *Martha's Vineyard Magazine*, September 1, 2007. *Photo by Thomas Dresser.*

While the mill and baking business may not have proved an especially viable venture, the road did serve as a means of transport across the Vineyard, from Edgartown in the east to North Road on the western side of the Island, linking the villages of Middletown and West Tisbury with the county seat in Edgartown.

Toward the end of his life, Fisher became embroiled in a political discussion about construction of an alternate roadway from Edgartown to Middletown. Fisher wrote a letter to the *Vineyard Gazette* espousing his opinions, and it was published on March 13, 1874. Dr. Fisher claimed, "I repaired the Susan Allen route at an expense of about $3000 to make it passable." He complained of the potholes and steep hills on Manter's Road (the Mill Path) en route to his mill and added, "After using sometimes one and then the other, I abandoned the Manter road and repaired the Susan Allen road," which we have to assume became his road.

In his letter to the editor, years after his road was in place, Dr. Daniel Fisher protested any new construction. He wrote, "The road on which I now go to the mill is about two-and-a-half miles farther than to go on a straight line and is the best." He acknowledged that his road was longer but claimed that it was more convenient and likely safer as well.

Sections of the road spilled out of Edgartown along what is now the Edgartown–West Tisbury Road. Other sections followed the routes of ancient ways. The road was completed in 1860, and for the next fifteen or twenty years, wagonloads of ground wheat or corn were hauled nearly ten miles by horse-drawn wagons across the Great Plain (now the state forest) to Edgartown. The hardtack was baked, packed and sold to whaling captains setting forth on their ventures. Dr. Fisher's effort was enterprising and exemplified the expansive vision of this nineteenth-century Renaissance Vineyarder.

Daniel Webster visited the Vineyard in 1849 and affirmed its beauty and charm. Webster accompanied Dr. Fisher in a horse-drawn wagon rumbling along the road across the Great Plain, "shooting plover from a carriage. Dr. Fisher was a better marksman from the moving vehicle."[23]

Daniel Fisher died in 1876. His mill closed shortly thereafter, and the structure was removed to Vineyard Haven to become the Crocker Harness Factory.

Finding Dr. Fisher's Road

The Dr. Fisher Road runs nearly ten miles out of Edgartown, first along the Edgartown–West Tisbury Road. Near Andrea's Auto (formerly McIntosh Motors), the Road veers off into the woods, heading northwest into the middle of the Island, through what is now the state forest. From the headquarters of the state forest, the road crosses Barnes Road just north of the Frisbee Golf Course, meets and follows along the paved bicycle path and emerges onto Old County Road adjacent to the West Tisbury School.

The final link is about a half mile in length, beginning by a signpost that denotes the Dr. Fisher Road off Old County Road and exits onto Old Stage Road, thence parallel and adjacent to State Road, where it angles southwest. "Finally the wagon would have turned onto North Road, arriving a few minutes later at the Fisher Mill [Crocker Mill], where the horses would have had a chance to drink from the cool mill pond."[24] There, the wagon would be loaded with grain for the return trip to Edgartown.

This cross-Island transit system was in operation by 1860 and continued until Dr. Fisher's death in 1876. No records indicate that the mill was in use after 1880. A newspaper account from the 1870s reported that Dr. Fisher hired seventy men to perform substantial repairs to his road. Over the years, the Road was a reliable route for people walking or riding between the east and west villages of the Vineyard, across the Great Plain; it was in use at least until 1900, the dawn of the automotive age.

The *Vineyard Gazette*, on September 27, 1940, characterized Fisher's efforts on his road, "which he got permission to build from the authorities of the towns, is still passable in places, and has been known since he built it as the Dr. Fisher's Road. It was a fine dirt road when he finished it, over which his four-horse trams could be driven at a gallop."

Today, Dr. Fisher's Road lives on in various incarnations. The route runs across the Island in an arc across level grassy plains of what is now the state forest. The area is accessible today from the state forest to the mill on North Road. Motor vehicles are not permitted, but walkers, joggers and bicyclists enjoy access for miles along most of the open route. The Fisher Road is 6.5 miles through the woods and 3.5 miles on paved roads.

Historian Bow Van Riper of the Martha's Vineyard Museum observed that the Dr. Fisher Road is

> *one of fifteen officially designated "ancient ways" on the Island, and (like most roads with that designation) it wasn't necessarily "built" in the*

way we think of the term so much as it was worn into the landscape by continued use over the course of decades. It would have been a cart track in those days, of course, and while people probably would have done incidental maintenance—clearing fallen trees, cutting back low-hanging branches, and maybe filling particularly troublesome holes with dirt or gravel—I doubt there would have been concerted efforts to maintain or improve it.[25]

From west to east, I began to explore the Dr. Fisher Road on a warm November afternoon. Beginning off Old County Road in West Tisbury, I drove partway along the roadway marked Dr. Fisher Road, parked and walked the half-mile roadway through to Old Stage Road. Driveways access new houses nearby. The road runs through woods in a relatively straight line. At the far end, potholes, dips and depressions make it a challenge for an automobile. While I was on foot, two trucks passed me, easing their way along the roadway. I met one cyclist who chatted enthusiastically about how the road was a convenient route to the West Tisbury School from State Road.

The Dr. Fisher Road emerged onto Old Stage Road in West Tisbury adjacent to the infamous Dumptique. This last section can be navigated on foot or bicycle or in a four-wheel-drive vehicle, but I would not recommend it for regular traffic.

After this initial foray, I was hungry for more. I retraced my steps and parked across from the West Tisbury School on Old County Road. I immediately found myself on an ancient roadway, a straight cart-road, leading through the state forest. I walked along for about twenty minutes, going about a mile and a quarter, across an open field interrupted by low bushes. The road runs parallel to existing woods of the state forest. (Later, in consultation with Martha's Vineyard Commission senior planner Bill Veno, I learned that the road wiggles a bit. The fire road I walked is straight; the original road jogs a bit into the underbrush, identifiable in old maps and then straightens out into this section of the Dr. Fisher Road.)

I reached the paved bicycle path, a leg of the twelve-mile circuit around the airport. There I turned and retraced my steps, marveling at the tranquil ambulatory route, the open but secluded landscape and the sense of solitude in the midst of an island of eighteen thousand people. It was a peaceful hour on a delightful afternoon.

Not content to leave this section of the Road incompletely investigated, I drove around to Barnes Road at the state forest and put in across from the deer-check building on Sanderson Road. On crossing Barnes Road, I walked toward a roadway I'd spotted. As I approached, I was startled

Meandering along the Dr. Fisher Road is an opportunity to appreciate the wilderness still accessible on Martha's Vineyard. *Photo by Thomas Dresser.*

by the appearance of a young man exiting the roadway. I asked if this was the Dr. Fisher Road; he wasn't sure but told me it led to a bike path in a ten-minute walk. In a few minutes, I reached the paved bike path, a continuation of the same path that connects with the other end of the Road where I had been.

In short, I walked a mile and three-quarters, approaching the paved bike path from both directions; the missing link now was the mile-and-a-half path between the two ends. Discovering the easy access points to the Dr. Fisher Road was a most enjoyable addenda to a leisurely afternoon. Now I know.

The next day, I came with my bike. I put in by the West Tisbury School and pedaled along the rutted fire road that follows the Dr. Fisher Road. I reached the paved bike path quickly and rode along for ten minutes or so until I reached the spur of the road extending in from Barnes Road. Once I reached Barnes Road, I turned around, retracing my route. I had now completed two segments of the Dr. Fisher Road.

It was not until a couple of months after the deer-hunting season drew to a close that I was able to hike on the Dr. Fisher Road once more. The January day was unseasonably warm after a cold snap, so I was overdressed as I parked at the headquarters of the state forest and set off in a southeasterly direction on the next leg of the road.

For more than thirty minutes, I walked briskly along the Dr. Fisher Road. The middle was well-worn, more of a path, but the roadway was clear and wagon width. I passed through groves of white pine, pitch pine and scrub oak and an enchanting cluster of spruce trees, tall and majestic, laden with cones and bright green needles.

Along the way, I grew warm and gradually removed one layer after another but kept on my journey, crossing a couple of fire lanes, long and straight and open. I proceeded until a house interrupted my line of vision. And then another. I had walked clear across the heart of the state forest and passed just north of the development known as Bold Meadow. I continued until I reached a paved road with more houses, signs and moving vehicles and realized I was on Metcalf Drive, and that was my end point for the day.

It took about an hour and a quarter to complete the jaunt, over and back. I was alone, walking at a good pace, and felt invigorated that I had added another link in the cross-Island chain known as Dr. Fisher Road. After consultation and computation with the Whiting map of 1850, I figured I walked nearly two miles along the road; I still have miles to go in the final segment, but I'm making progress.

On a mild late January day, my wife, Joyce, and I walked through the Land Bank's Pennywise Preserve off the Edgartown–Vineyard Haven Road. At the most southern point, we came to the juncture of Three Cornered Rock Road where it intersected with the Dr. Fisher Road, east of Metcalf Drive. We walked briskly along that section of the road, confirming its intersection with Metcalf Drive. We had added another section to the road and another access point, as Sheriff's Meadow property abuts the Dr. Fisher Road at the southern point of the Vineyard Golf Course just off Metcalf Drive. It's all coming together.

As Tod Dimmick summarized his experience for *Martha's Vineyard Magazine* some years ago, "The ability to walk for six miles in a straight shot of relative wilderness is rare on the Island and it's part of the magic of the Dr. Fisher Road."[26]

The Town of Edgartown defined the Dr. Fisher Road as a District of Critical Planning Concern (DCPC), meaning it cannot be developed and public access must be maintained. Upkeep is not part of the stipulation, however, so the road may become overgrown in places and hard to follow along parts of the route.

Today, a third of the road runs along a paved roadway or bike path in the state forest. The original road is passable and clearly denoted on numerous maps. With minimal effort, one can navigate the length of the entire roadway. What an adventure!

Primitive roadways were typical of mid-century Martha's Vineyard, where a journey from one part of the Island to another "meant crossing somewhat desolate stretches of scrub and woods on frequently miserable roadways that were regularly disparaged in contemporary accounts." When Nathaniel Shaler, of Kentucky, sought to reach his summer retreat, he had to open and close an eponymous seven gates before he got to his house. And one annoyed traveler complained about "the opening and closing some thirty fence gates as he traveled from West Tisbury to Gay Head"[27] in 1838. The gates or bars restricted roaming sheep and cattle that predominated the landscape. Consequently, the gates made travel by horse or horse and buggy both tedious and time-consuming.

Dr. Fisher's was not the only roadway that evolved on the Vineyard in the nineteenth century. Several other roads emerged from trails and paths, and some were eventually paved. We think of Middle Road, created in 1845; North Road, laid out in 1849; State Road in Gay Head, in 1850; and the Edgartown–Holmes Hole (Vineyard Haven) Road, also in 1850. (When this roadway improvement qualified for federal funds in the 1960s, it was widened to become the Vineyard's first "highway.")

Other roadway improvements in the mid- to late nineteenth century included construction of the bridge across the Lagoon, which opened in 1871, and the road between Edgartown and Cottage City along what is now known as State Beach, in 1872. (This route became known as the cheesecloth road, as the best way to build on sand at the time was to cover the sand with cheesecloth.) The Dr. Fisher Road was never paved across the Vineyard but lingers today as a testament to nineteenth-century horse-and-wagon transport across the Island.

Chapter 4

STEAMSHIP SERVICE COMES OF AGE

1860-1900

Wesleyan Grove now draws its thousands from the whole populous east of the United States, and stragglers from afar. It is known all over the country—no, all over the world. It is the largest and most famous of all the camp meetings, and its fame is growing."[28] By the mid-nineteenth century, the Martha's Vineyard Camp Meeting Association was attracting throngs from around the world. And how did they reach Cottage City? By steamship. On one day in 1860, *Eagle's Wing* brought 1,200 participants and *Island Home* another 1,400. This was a bustling business.

The side-wheeler *Monohansett* (1862–86) was designed and built by Captain Benjamin Cromwell, the former captain of the *Eagle's Wing*. The *Monohansett* began service to the Vineyard but was soon requisitioned for the war effort. The *Monohansett* proved one of the more popular Vineyard steamboats, earning the fierce loyalty of discerning Islanders. Its crew had a Vineyard makeup, with Captain Cromwell at the helm and Mate Hiram Crowell and Purser John Mayhew from Edgartown—significantly fewer crew members than on today's vessels.

During the Civil War, the United States government paid $500 per day to charter the *Monohansett* in the war effort. The *Monohansett* was used to transport dispatches to Union ships off the Outer Banks in North Carolina and transport troops off Hilton Head, South Carolina. Later, the vessel was used in the Potomac.

To cover the absence of the *Monohansett* on Vineyard Sound during the war, the *Helen Augusta* was introduced but proved inadequate due to its

The *Monohansett* was a dependable side-wheeler for Martha's Vineyard. The steamship served in the Union navy and later brought revivalists to camp meetings. *Courtesy of Chris Baer, history.vineyard.net/photos.*

limited space for passengers and freight and infrequent trips across the Sound (only thrice a week). The *Helen Augusta* was not a popular substitute for the *Monohansett.*

During the war years and beyond, various steamships transported an increasing number of revivalists to the Camp Meeting Association in Cottage City. Vessels such as the *Helen Augusta*, the *Canonicus*, *Island Home* and even the *Monohansett*, during intermittent breaks in war service, were used to transport enthusiasts to Wesleyan Grove for the revival meetings. On Sunday, August 28, 1863, the *Monohansett* brought 1,400 passengers over to the Vineyard in the morning and transferred 1,800 back that evening. These were boatloads of fervent believers. And in what must have been a harrowing trip in the summer of 1865, 2,200 passengers squeezed aboard the *Monohassett*, creating a dangerously overloaded vessel. Fortunately, nothing untoward occurred.

Tourism became a natural outgrowth of the revivalist movement. Promotional guides for Martha's Vineyard were ripe with enthusiastic declarations of Vineyard wonders. "The bathing facilities are excellent," crowed one booklet, reveling in the fine fishing and the safe, friendly atmosphere. "Large steamers pass and repass several times a day, while the ocean is oftentimes literally covered with sailing craft of almost every description; from the small pleasure-yacht to the noble merchantman, with her cloud of snowy canvas."[29]

As with earlier steamers, towing ships in distress was another source of revenue. On one memorable venture, the *Monohansett* rescued the schooner *William F. Garrison*, which became hung up on the rocky shore of Nomans Land. After a bit of legal wrangling, the owners of the schooner paid the handsome sum of $1,700 to the steamship company for rescuing their vessel.

After the war, the *Monohansett* returned to service for the Vineyard until 1886. In 1902, it was used as an excursion vessel north of Boston and was wrecked on Misery Island off Salem Harbor in 1904.

Following the Civil War, railroads assumed a larger role in transportation all across America. The transcontinental railroad connected East and West in 1869. In southeastern Massachusetts, Old Colony Railroad expanded its holdings, buying up smaller lines until it owned twenty-three individual companies and oversaw more than six hundred miles of track. Railway service was extended from Boston to Hyannis, on Cape Cod, in 1854; to Woods Hole in Falmouth in 1872; and to New Bedford the next year.

Due to its proximity to Boston, Woods Hole evolved into a key port for steamers to transport passengers across the Sound to the Vineyard. Steamship companies recognized that to dock in Woods Hole was closer to Boston than New Bedford; hence, more passengers could be transported more efficiently. Steamships to Nantucket switched from Hyannis to Woods Hole for the closer train terminus in 1872. (Service returned to Hyannis for the Nantucket boats in 1984.)

Shortly after the Civil War, plans were made to improve and expand steamship docking on the Vineyard. A dock was projected for Eastville on East Chop. The Eastville Dock was completed in 1866. However, revivalists who debarked in Eastville faced a walk of more than a mile to the Camp Meeting Association, an unappealing marketing point. Discussion ensued to provide trolley service from the harbor to the Camp Meeting Association. The Eastville Dock regained prominence toward the end of the century when the New York Yacht Club sailed into Vineyard Haven Harbor, moored dozens of sailing vessels off Eastville and took full advantage of that dock. By then, trolleys, first horse-drawn and then electric, serviced this area.

The Oak Bluffs Land and Wharf Company built a new pier in downtown Cottage City in 1867, adjacent to its extensive land development project. It was at the site of the present pier in use today by the Steamship Authority in Oak Bluffs. Regularly scheduled steamship service was diverted to this new dock.

The Vineyard Grove Company constructed a third pier, Highland Wharf, in Cottage City in 1871 specifically for the Methodist Camp Meeting Association. Highland Wharf was adjacent to the Highland Hotel at the site of the present East Chop Beach Club. This pier was used by the Camp Meeting Association as well as patrons of the Baptist Tabernacle in the Highlands. "The purpose was symbolic, to allow those destined for the campground to disembark with dignity via a route especially designed to circumvent the more worldly parts of this growing resort community."[30]

"Steamers from other areas [such as Maine and New York] often visited the wharves on Martha's Vineyard. They would come for day excursions or with charters. Passengers on these trips could see the sights on the island or attend the Methodist or Baptist camp meetings."[31]

Another popular excursion aboard steamboats was to take tourists from Cottage City out to Gay Head, where day-trippers would ride in ox carts, admire the multicolored clay cliffs and view the brick lighthouse. This service brought tourist dollars to cash-strapped Gay Head, which was isolated from the rest of the island due to inadequate roadways and the long distance. People in Gay Head found it faster to do their shopping in New Bedford. Sailing across Buzzards Bay and back was more efficient than the twenty-mile horse-drawn wagon ride to and from Holmes Hole.

One of the more historic steamships to ply Vineyard Sound was the *River Queen* (1864–80s). For much of its tenure, G.L. Daggett of Holmes Hole was captain. The *River Queen* was much appreciated by the postwar Vineyard population.

Like the *Monohansett*, the *River Queen* was called into service during the Civil War as a private dispatch boat for General Ulysses S. Grant on the Potomac.

When President Grant visited Martha's Vineyard in August 1874, he rode a three-car train provided by the Old Colony Railroad, which had recently

The Active pulls out of Cottage City as the *River Queen* prepares to steam across Vineyard Sound. President Grant arrived on Martha's Vineyard in 1874 aboard the *River Queen*. *Courtesy of Martha's Vineyard Antique Photos.*

extended service to Woods Hole. From there, President Grant and his party crossed Vineyard Sound aboard the *River Queen*, landing at the Highland Wharf. Grant boarded the horse-drawn trolley to ride into the grounds of the Camp Meeting Association. Aboard the *River Queen*, President Grant reportedly said:

> *"I remember that this is the boat we had when the commissioners of the Confederacy met Lincoln and myself to try to effect peace." There is no exact record of this anecdote, as Grant proceeded to tell it; but the circumstances are too apt and characteristic to be far from historical fact. Alexander H. Stephens, Grant went on to say, was one of the leaders of the Confederacy, and he was a diminutive man. As the discussion in the small cabin of the old* River Queen *waxed hot, Stephens peeled off one coat, then another, and then another. Lincoln looked at him, Grant said, and remarked, "That's the smallest ear for the biggest shuck I ever saw."*[32]

After his brief tenure on the Vineyard, the president boarded the *Monohansett* en route to New Bedford and the train ride back to Washington.

The *River Queen* plied Vineyard Sound well into the 1880s. After service to the Vineyard was discontinued, the *River Queen* returned, ironically, to the Potomac River. It was there, in 1911, that the vessel suffered an ignoble demise when a signal lantern exploded, causing the steamer to burst into flames and sink.

The fastest steamship of the Vineyard fleet of the late nineteenth century was the *Martha's Vineyard* (1871–1900) of the New Bedford, Vineyard and Nantucket Steamboat Company. Speed secured the place of the *Martha's Vineyard* in the annals of Island history. It made a historic run from the Camp Meeting Association to New Bedford in an hour and a half. Another record was in place for twenty years: New Bedford to Nantucket in three and three-quarters hours. This was one fast steamship.

For three decades, the *Martha's Vineyard* was a workhorse for the steamship company. However, by 1900, it had been demoted to a spare boat and was used primarily for short junkets, such as the occasional excursion to Gay Head. It sank after collision with a steam lighter in 1916.

During this era, an issue arose about a steamship whistle. Citizens of Vineyard Haven promulgated a petition to protest "loud and prolonged ringing of bells and the screeching of whistles in the early morning." This unseemly noise at dawn was deemed "unnecessary." There is no record of the response from the steamship company.[33]

In 1886, the competing island steamship companies of Martha's Vineyard and Nantucket reached a rapprochement with their complementary goals. The two operations merged to form a single corporation under a single management umbrella to provide improved service for both islands.

The largest shareholder in the new New Bedford, Martha's Vineyard and Nantucket Steamboat Company was the Old Colony Railroad. The new company consolidated service to the three ports and added two new steamships to its fleet.

The first vessel built by the revamped company was the *Nantucket* (1886–1913). This ship drew only four and a half feet of water, while other vessels had a draught of six feet. Hence, the *Nantucket* could cross the sandbar off Nantucket Harbor. The *Nantucket* succeeded the popular *Island Home* and proved a speedy and seaworthy vessel. According to the local press, "She made the run to Cottage City in two hours and thirty minutes, and 'worked like a charm.'"

The *Nantucket* was sold in 1913 and continued service as a freight boat but was wrecked and sank in the Hudson River in 1919.

Built in 1891, the 701-ton, 203-foot-long *Gay Head* (1891–1924) was the largest steamship of the new fleet. The social hall was 50 feet long; cherry seats upholstered in maroon velvet added to the allure. An elaborate carved staircase led from one deck to another. Black walnut and maple defined the interior, adorned with gold paint. A passionate review rhapsodied, "No description can convey an idea of the beauties of this craft; the grace and symmetry of the whole steamer which is apparent from the waterline to the tip of her shining smoke stack. The convenience of her accommodations and furnishings must all be seen to be appreciated."[34] Both conventional oil lamps and nascent electric lights were in operation, and gallons of drinking water were provided to quench the passengers' thirst.

On a foggy day in Vineyard Sound, the *Gay Head* collided with the *Nantucket*. No one was injured, although both ships sustained damage. In another accident, the *Martha's Vineyard* ran aground off Nantucket in 1900 and had to be towed off. The *Monohansett* was unsuccessful in rescuing its sister ship, but the *Gay Head* succeeded.

The *Gay Head* was taken out of service in 1924. Plans were made but never realized to convert it to a floating dance hall. It was deactivated and sank off New York City in the early 1930s.

As the whaling industry fell into decline, both Nantucket and Martha's Vineyard assumed new roles. Nantucket promoted itself as a health resort, while the Vineyard encouraged the tourist crowd.

Martha's Vineyard segued from a whaling port to a vacation destination, welcoming summer people as well as day-trippers. The Vineyard became recognized as an idyllic tourist attraction. On occasion, steamers from Providence or New York City would dock at Eastville en route to their eventual port. Cottage City earned a reputation as a burgeoning summer resort.

The Vineyard was evolving.

Chapter 5

HORSE-DRAWN TROLLEY CARS

1873–1895

Shortly after landscape architect Robert Morris Copeland prepared detailed plans for the planned community of the Oak Bluffs Land and Wharf Company in 1867, the aggressive land development organization expressed its intentions to meet the needs of its customer base. Erastus Carpenter, the motivator behind the Oak Bluffs Land and Wharf Company, worked with the Old Colony Railroad to extend the track to Woods Hole. That was key to promoting his new development. He also instigated construction of a new pier in Cottage City adjacent to his new development.

As noted, the Old Colony Railroad line was completed from Boston to Woods Hole in 1872. (Service was discontinued in 1964.) Train service was convenient for Bostonians who wanted to visit the Vineyard, and steamship service quickly accommodated passengers who arrived at Woods Hole by train. With train service to Woods Hole and ferry service across Vineyard Sound, a need arose to provide trolley service to transport those passengers who reached Cottage City.

In 1870, the Vineyard Grove Company drew up plans for a horsecar route from the Highland House Wharf to the Camp Meeting Association. Methodist revivalists wanted to go directly to Wesleyan Grove, the Methodist campground on the shores of Sunset Lake.

A trolley track would run from the Highland Wharf at the present East Chop Beach Club to Trinity Park in the Camp Meeting Association grounds. The mile-long track was laid out, and horsecar service began operation in 1873. The horsecar consisted of an open wagon pulled along the track by a pair of horses. The wagon had a curved roof over benches, with rolled curtains to be lowered as protection against rain.

The horse-drawn trolley system was known as the Oak Bluffs Street Railway Company and began operations, summers only, in 1873. Profit for its first summer was $465 from the sale of more than forty thousand tickets.

The route of the horsecar was designed to meet the needs of the Methodist Camp Meeting Association. It picked up passengers and their luggage right out on the steamship pier and delivered them directly to the campground, thus avoiding the attractions and distractions of Cottage City, which ranged from dance halls to bowling alleys, from a toboggan slide to a roller-skating rink. The amusement park atmosphere was so close the fear was that it would entice wayward Methodists, hence the isolated Highland Wharf and the unique horse-drawn trolley route into Wesleyan Grove. And for those patrons who sought to indulge in the vagaries of bathing beaches, ice cream parlors and candy shops, the steamboat wharf was less than a half mile distant, at the end of Circuit Avenue. In an effort to restrict Methodists from imbibing or frequenting the forbidden pleasures of Circuit Avenue, or to curtail curious non-Methodists from impinging on campground sermons, a seven-foot-high stockade was erected around the Camp Meeting Association grounds prior to 1870.

The carts or wagons of the street railway were housed in a car barn on the harbor, not far from the present East Chop Beach Club. Today, an apartment building stands on the site overlooking the harbor; it may well have been part of the railway system all those years ago.

The horse-drawn trolley track ran along Eastville Avenue, turned onto New York Avenue by the present Our Market and "crossed the River Jordan" by Sunset Lake. At the time, Oak Bluffs Harbor was a freshwater lake called Squash Meadow Pond; later, it became Lake Anthony. It was dredged out and opened to create Oak Bluffs Harbor in 1900. At Sunset Lake, the track turned sharply to the right, down Dukes County Avenue, close to the campground cottages along Siloam Avenue and into Trinity Park, which it circled, then returned to the Highland Wharf, making a figure nine. Cost of the ride was six cents.

The horse-drawn trolley gained national prominence in 1874.

No doubt the most famous passenger to ride this first line was President Ulysses S. Grant, who in August 1874 rode a festooned car behind six horses into the Camp Ground to stay with Bishop Gilbert Haven at his

The track for the horse trolley led into the Martha's Vineyard Camp Meeting Association. *Courtesy of Martha's Vineyard Antique Photos.*

cottage on Clinton Avenue. Grant and his retinue, which included his wife, had arrived at Highland Wharf aboard the steamer River Queen, *once President Lincoln's private yacht but by then in Vineyard service.*[35]

In 1879, the Camp Meeting Association constructed the wrought-iron open-air Tabernacle or religious chapel to replace the massive canvas canopy that had been erected annually over the benches for the patrons of the association. Iron sections of the Tabernacle were shipped by ferry to the Highland Pier, then transported to the building site at Trinity Park on the horse-drawn wagons.

The horse-drawn trolley transported revivalists and their luggage past gingerbread cottages into Trinity Park. *Courtesy of Martha's Vineyard Antique Photos.*

The success of the horsecar trolley continued for twenty years. In the early 1890s, the street railway expanded in several directions. The most obvious route was to plan a subsidiary trolley track into Vineyard Haven, but that failed to materialize.

A much more ambitious horsecar route was promoted in 1891. The trolley line would run from Circuit Avenue in Cottage City over the Lagoon Bridge through Tisbury to connect at the wharf in Lambert's Cove with steamships to New York. The line would continue all the way to Chilmark and on to Gay Head. This proposed trolley line would extend twenty-five miles, linking up-Island with the down-Island communities. The plan of the Oak Bluffs Street Railway Company was promoted by three prominent Vineyarders: Charles Strahan, Henry Whiting and Nathaniel Shaler. While the suggested line was never built, the promoters believed that the idea of a trolley ride out to Gay Head through Vineyard scenery would attract tourists. (This promotion is still in play today. Sightseers board tour buses, which lumber through miles of woods out to Aquinnah.)

The plan for a trolley line out to Gay Head was never realized, even when the trolley service was electrified in 1895. Nevertheless, on Eldridge's 1913 map of Martha's Vineyard, the proposed electric railway track runs all the way out to Gay Head.

In 1892, the horse railroad was extended along New York Avenue to Eastville. This addition was a profitable trolley line as the New York Yacht

Club built a structure on the Eastville Pier. This horse-trolley line out to Eastville opened on June 15, 1892, and was quite popular, with cars running every half hour. The Eastville Inn, near the present Martha's Vineyard Hospital, generated additional business with passengers. This line met patrons at the Eastville Pier, the original landing built years earlier.

The most ambitious addition to the horsecar line was track added to Lagoon Heights, also in 1892. That line began at the steamship wharf in Cottage City (the present Steamship Authority wharf), proceeded along Ocean Park on Sea View Avenue and turned in and up and through Waban Park. The trolley track route can be discerned running through Waban/ Dennis Alley Park by a line of cedar trees parallel to the original trolley track.

The line continued through Nashawena Park to Circuit Avenue, along Wing Road out to Alpine Avenue, concluding at the Prospect House, a hotel on the corner of Hudson and Beacon Streets in Lagoon Heights. Additionally, the line was extended down to the Lagoon itself to meet the needs of bathers on the shore of the Lagoon.

Horsecars ran every quarter hour, connecting passengers from Lagoon Heights to the Eastville Pier, with a transfer at Circuit Avenue, for a nickel. To travel from one part of Cottage City to another via trolley was very successful. Tourists appreciated the trolley service, especially as it connected with the steamships. This system met the needs of patrons up to the twentieth century, when automobiles brought major transformation to the landscape.

In the 1890s, the Oak Bluffs Street Railway became the Cottage City Street Railway Company.

Chapter 6

THE ERA OF THE ELECTRIC TROLLEY CAR

1895–1917

Electrification became so advanced by the end of the nineteenth century that it was applied to horse-drawn trolleys with little or no difficulty. The Cottage City Street Railway Company electrified all horsecars on its route, with the exception of the Trinity Park loop into the Camp Meeting Association. The transition from horsecar to electric power occurred abruptly in 1895.

The electrification program became possible with the purchase and installation of a generator that produced 150 horsepower to run the cars. The generator was installed at the corner of Eastville and Beach Roads in Oak Bluffs, near the present Martha's Vineyard Hospital.

An issue arose over use of utility poles by the electric trolley, the telephone company and the electric company. The problem was resolved, and the electrification program was successfully implemented. Soon, the electric trolley eclipsed the success of the horse-drawn trolley in speed and efficiency.

On a single day, Sunday, July 28, 1895, one electrified trolley car transported 803 passengers, and that day the entire system moved more than 2,500 people.

The Cottage City Street Railway ran only in the summer months but proved a profitable enterprise. In 1895, its first year of operation, the railway realized a profit of $5,381 from an income of $8,861, with expenses of $3,480. The inventory consisted of three electric boxcars or passenger cars and four electrified open cars; in subsequent years, the company purchased one boxcar and two open cars.

Profit produced promise. In the spring of 1895, the Boston and Quincy Railway Company purchased the Cottage City Street Railway. The new company built a high-end power station in Eastville with top-of-the-line electrical equipment. Plans for a route between Cottage City and Holmes Hole were underway. An additional profit center was realized when the line incorporated the track into Eastville and the stub line down to the New York Yacht Club pier along East Chop.

A two-person crew was required to run the electric trolley. The motorman ran the car and handled the mechanics of electrification. The conductor collected fares, dealt with passengers, organized freight and dropped the curtains in inclement weather.

Electric trolley cars could go in either direction. "There were electric controls on either end, and to reverse the car when stopped, the motorman got off and moved to the other end of the car with his controller handle. The conductor's job was to change the trolley pole so that it would be at the operating rear of the car."[36] The conductor pulled a rope, which connected the trolley pole to the overhead power wire. Then he walked to the rear of the car and released the rope so the pole reconnected to the wire that bore the electricity. Once he released the pole, the car received power from the electric cable and could proceed in the reverse direction.

Gene Baer described the flexibility of the trolley and how accommodating the crew was when he shared the story of a young girl named Ida Karl. Riding the open-air trolley, Miss Karl dropped a ball of yarn out of the moving car. The conductor caught her look of dismay and notified the motorman, who stopped the trolley. "The motorman smiled, nodded his head, and then stepped to the ground taking his controller [operating handle] with him. The conductor quickly reversed the trolley pole and jumped back on board as the motorman took the helm at

A reenactor at the Seashore Trolley Museum in Kennebunk, Maine, assumes the role of a nineteenth-century conductor aboard a trolley car. *Photo by Joyce Dresser.*

Conductor and motorman stand by an electric trolley car in Oak Bluffs. *Courtesy of the Connie Sanborn collection.*

the opposite end of the car."[37] Ida Karl retrieved her ball of yarn, and the trolley reversed direction once more.

Trolley cars were equipped with air brakes and an emergency hand brake. The motorman adjusted the speed with his controller handle. Most cars had open sides, with seven or eight benches across the car. The car itself was attached to a chassis called a truck, which had four wheels. Some cars were larger—not only longer but also running on a double set of trucks or wheels. Each car had a roof with curtains to be lowered in rainy weather.

Trolley cars were painted distinctive colors to attract attention. For example, Car #22 was painted gray with a green roof, maroon body and yellow trim. The running board, where the conductor stood to collect tickets, was gray as well. Larger cars had up to a dozen benches and accommodated up to sixty passengers.

An electric trolley car glides along New York Avenue, Oak Bluffs. *Courtesy of Martha's Vineyard Antique Photos.*

The diary of eighteen-year-old John Tingley vividly captures the life of a conductor on the Cottage City Street Railway. On June 24, 1895, Tingley was hired and trained and handed a railway cap; he had to provide the rest of his uniform, whatever he chose. His responsibilities, which began that first day, were to collect fares, assist passengers and move the trolley pole when the car reversed direction. He was exhausted after his first full day of work.

He recorded his summer experience of working on the railway, along with an appreciation for the entertainment afforded a young man in Cottage City. Tingley's diary entry for August 3, 1895, described the long hours and relevant observations: "Saturday. 1004 passengers, 958 cash fares; worked 8 am to 11 pm. The New York yacht club came in today and that accounts for the large increase of passengers. I saw the *Defender*, *Vigilant*, *Jubilee* and Vanderbilt's steam yacht *Valiant*. It is said that this is the largest fleet of yachts ever brought together."

Tingley was not scheduled to work during the day on Saturday, September 2. He enjoyed an excursion aboard the steamer *Columbia* out to Gay Head:

We started from Cottage City at 10 am, touched at Makonikey Heights, (Lambert's Cove) and arrived at Gay Head at 12 noon. We left at 2 pm, touched at Makonikey, and then ran over to Woods Hole to land some passengers. We arrived at Cottage City at 5:30 pm. We saw a large swordfish on the way back. There were about 44 in the party.

Tingley then went to work on his shift as conductor on the electric railway from 6:45 p.m. to 10:45 p.m., handling eighty-eight passengers. Sounds like a long day.

Tingley recorded his busiest day that summer, August 9, 1895, when the electric trolley transported 1,214 passengers; his slowest day was June 25, right after he started, with a mere 27 fares. Total passengers on his route in the course of the summer numbered 28,800. As well as putting in the long hours, Tingley was meticulous in his numerical recordings.

On June 25, 1898, the Prospect House Hotel in Lagoon Heights burned to the ground. The trolley line to that hotel was curtailed and shut down. The result was that the Cottage City Railway lost nearly $1,000 by 1901. In order to expand business, the railway company sought permission to lease, own and operate self-propelled vehicles, or automobiles, basically competing against itself.

By 1901, the railway company had fallen on more rough times. It was no longer popular nor profitable. The company sought to increase income with a land development scheme to develop a section of East Chop called Windermere, near the present nursing home by the same name, and authorize the sale of house lots. The plan was never realized.

Years earlier, in 1889, the Martha's Vineyard Street Railway Company was formed to lay track and operate trolleys in Vineyard Haven. Like the Cottage City line, it only ran in the summer. When it eventually began service in 1896, it had a terminal at the steamship wharf on Water Street, Vineyard Haven. The track ran down Water Street, through Five Corners and out along Beach Road, where its powerhouse was located. (The powerhouse provided electricity for the towns of Vineyard Haven and Edgartown but not Cottage City.) The trolley barn was across from the powerhouse on the Lagoon, on the grounds currently owned by R.M. Packer. The barn was destroyed by the hurricane of 1938.

On the Vineyard Haven side, the Martha's Vineyard Street Railway Company car ran as far as the bridge over the Lagoon. On the other side, the Cottage City Street Railway line likewise stopped at the bridge. As Herman Page wrote, "In the days when the trolley lines were first built, the bridge was not strong enough to bear the weight of both track and trolley cars."[38] Passengers were required to disembark and walk across the bridge; hopefully a car from the other line would be there to meet them.

If the next trolley had not yet arrived when passengers disembarked, they were encouraged to visit the Eagleston Tea House, "perched close to the sea on the Tisbury side of the bridge. This picturesque stop became for many an outing in itself."[39] The Tea House met the gastronomical delights of passengers who had to wait for the competing trolley. Thus, the bridge served as a literal dividing line between the two trolley lines. The Eagleston Tea House was destroyed in the hurricane of 1944.

Trolley cars could not safely cross the drawbridge until it was rebuilt. Passengers disembarked to wait for the connecting trolley. *Courtesy of Martha's Vineyard Antique Photos.*

Car #31 at the Seashore Trolley Museum is similar to trolley cars purchased by the Oak Bluffs Street Railway Company. *Photo by Joyce Dresser.*

The Martha's Vineyard Street Railway, located in Vineyard Haven, operated two cars, one heated for passenger comfort. The company controlled 1.1 miles of track, from the present Steamship Pier to the drawbridge. In 1902, the line transported 21,742 passengers, bustling along at eight miles per hour. The *Vineyard Gazette* of January 22, 1903, reported that the Martha's Vineyard Street Railway Company, "hoped to absorb the Cottage City Street Railway through purchase of the lease, so as to obviate necessity of laying new tracks there."

Subsequent plans included a line to Edgartown from Cottage City; however, funding could not be raised, and Edgartown was left to its own devices.

It was reported that the selectmen in Vineyard Haven voted to build a new drawbridge, one strong enough for trolley cars to cross.

While efforts were proposed to merge the Martha's Vineyard Street Railway with the Cottage City Street Railway Company, nothing succeeded until an aggressive action occurred: the Vineyard Haven company literally "cut off electricity to the Oak Bluffs company, leaving several cars carrying passengers stranded on the line."[40] That defiant action propelled the two companies into a merger in 1906, forming the Oak Bluffs Street Railway Company. This new conglomerate operated for two and a half months each summer over 6.5 miles of track. It boasted a fleet of eight enclosed cars, seven open cars and seven motorcars. A new car was purchased in 1906, adding to the inventory.

In 1912, the Oak Bluffs Street Railway Company extended its electrification along Siloam Avenue and into the campground, thus electrifying its entire line.

For many people, the trolley brought back fond memories. Riders could "recall with nostalgic affection the comings and goings, the clanging and rocking of these old open-air trolley cars," wrote Gene Baer in his tribute to the trolley cars of Martha's Vineyard. At the time, consumers considered the electric trolley car as the roadway to the future, but that was not to be.

Competition to the electric railway service came from several sources at the dawn of the twentieth century. "Already the first automobiles were arriving by boat from the mainland, and for those who could see the future, the trolley as a means of transportation was destined to become as dated as the creaking schooners that were still plying Vineyard Sound."[41] The automobile emerged as the most obvious threat.

Gasoline-engine motored jitneys also competed with the electric trolley for passengers. Jitneys were wildcat taxis that covered the same ground (and much more) than a trolley in half the time and half the price. The ride in a jitney from Oak Bluffs to Edgartown was twenty-five cents, and the trolley did not even go there. The demise of the Oak Bluffs Street Railway occurred at the end of the summer of 1918, at the end of World War I.

Rails from the electric trolley line were taken up and loaded aboard the *Alice S. Wentworth*. Captain Zeb Tilton sailed the *Wentworth* to Chester, Pennsylvania, where the rails were sold as scrap. "It is befitting," wrote historian Baer, "that the rails of this old open-car trolley line should be carried away in a colorful old schooner which was in itself a proud relic of another age."[42] One of the old trolley cars was converted into a diner in Vineyard Haven, owned and operated by Ornam Slocum, brother of Joshua Slocum, the first man to sail around the world single-handedly. (Its current location is unknown.)

Finding the Electric Trolley

Remnants of the street railway system are minimal. A section of track was preserved in front of the Camp Meeting Association headquarters to memorialize the traditional means of transport to the campground in the late nineteenth century. Two lengths of rail are embedded in the pavement not far from the Tabernacle. It is likely the only track extant from the trolley.

A tourist guidebook from 1932 contains these intriguing words: "Two of the old street railroad cars may be seen on the side of the road leading from Vineyard Haven toward Gay Head and other towns. These cars are now used for summer cottages."[43] Their location is unknown.

Stan Lair sits on the remains of an old trolley car, circa 1980. *Courtesy of Chris Baer, history. vineyard.net/photos.*

A section of the original trolley track was embedded by the headquarters of the Camp Meeting Association building in Trinity Park. *Photo by Joyce Dresser.*

Big Dipper serves ice cream in the building that used to be the waiting room for passengers of the Cottage City Street Railway Company. *Photo by Joyce Dresser.*

The only building still standing from the Cottage City Street Railway Company is at the foot of Circuit Avenue. This structure was once a waiting room or station for the railway; now it houses an ice cream parlor. In years gone by, it was a transfer station for passengers to change trolleys.

Chapter 7

THE MARTHA'S VINEYARD RAILROAD

1874–1895

The Martha's Vineyard Railroad was born of jealousy, fueled by fear and developed through desperation. Businessmen of Edgartown wanted a piece of the financial pie provided by the tourist industry in Cottage City. Townspeople feared the people of Cottage City, which was part of Edgartown, would secede. Edgartown businessmen sought an economic replacement for their declining whaling industry.

Thus, the Martha's Vineyard Railroad was "partially financed by the town [Edgartown], its purpose was to attract business from the boom-town of Oak Bluffs to the new and struggling resort hotel near Edgartown's South Beach."[44]

With the financial assistance of Erastus Carpenter of Oak Bluffs and Dr. Daniel Fisher of Edgartown, Old Colony Railroad extended its railroad line from Boston to Woods Hole in 1872. Now the Vineyard was more accessible to patrons from Boston. The side-wheelers *River Queen*, *Black Bird*, *Martha's Vineyard*, *Island Home* and *Monohansett* steamed between Woods Hole and Martha's Vineyard. The new wharves in Cottage City made steamship travel to the Vineyard more accessible.

A plethora of hotels blossomed in Cottage City in the 1870s to accommodate the hordes of tourists who arrived at the seaside community of Cottage City. The Wesley House, the Sea View House and the Highland House all stood right on the harbor; the Ocean View Hotel, the Pawnee House, the Metropolitan and the Island House were just inland. The Prospect House was a trolley ride away. Cottage City evolved into the center of tourism for Martha's Vineyard.

People of Edgartown sought a piece of the action. They wanted to entice off-Islanders to visit Edgartown to spend their money. The fear that Cottage City would act on the rumblings of secession from Edgartown were real. (And this fear was soon realized: Cottage City broke away from Edgartown in 1880.)

Two prominent Edgartownians spearheaded the group that advocated construction of a railroad. Whaling captain Nathanial Jernegan and whaleship owner Samuel Osborn Jr. viewed the railroad as a potential magnet to attract tourists to Edgartown. Tourism could supplement and eventually replace the dying whaling industry. Erstwhile entrepreneur Erastus Carpenter, of the Oak Bluffs Land and Wharf Company, strongly supported construction of the potential railroad.

Edgar Merchant, aged editor of the *Vineyard Gazette*, joined the march for the railroad to Edgartown. "When we have a railroad," he editorialized, "we shall see improvements made in our village never before thought of. The 'snort of the iron horse' will arouse men from their lethargy and infuse new life into their veins."[45]

"Edgartown, whose whaling industry had withered away by the early 1870s, coveted the vacationers who were crowding festive Oak Bluffs, in those days a satellite village of the town."[46] The financial Panic of 1873 frightened enough people to make an economic argument that the town needed to fund a railroad to entice tourists to Edgartown.

The argument continued:

> *A railroad was the only way to get the sporting types of Oak Bluffs to visit the decaying waterfront and somnambulant streets of Edgartown, and if that didn't make them regret the trip enough, perhaps to venture out to the prairie of Katama to have a clambake in their bowlers and neckties and see a hotel, the Mattakeset Lodge, that looked haunted even at noontime on a sunny summer's day.*[47]

The Katama Land and Wharf Company began construction of the Mattakeset Lodge on Katama Bay. A ferry wharf was built at South Beach. The Lodge, an elegant, elaborate seaside hotel, opened on August 1, 1873. Yet there was no adequate access to the Lodge or the beach in Katama.

Businessmen in Edgartown sought to build a railroad between Cottage City and Edgartown and thence out to Katama on the south shore. The

Katama Land and Wharf Company urged construction of a railroad; it was considered the best means to entice people to journey from Cottage City to Katama.

Whaling captain Nathaniel Jernegan served as sales agent for the company. Joseph Thaxter Pease, son of the founder of the Methodist campground, supported the effort. Erastus Carpenter was named president of the railroad. He had founded the Oak Bluffs Land and Wharf Company that constructed the Sea View House and worked closely on construction of the Mattakeset Lodge. The plan was to share the wealth of tourists who already enjoyed Cottage City with the business opportunities on the south shore of Katama in Edgartown. What could be easier than to link the two disparate parts of the town with a train, the most modern means of locomotion?

Ichabod Luce of Cottage City adamantly opposed the railroad. His argument was that it was the responsibility of the town to provide and maintain the schools and the roads and care for the indigent. Private business should pay for private projects, such as a railroad. Many townspeople agreed with Luce and considered the railroad a risky financial venture.

Editor Edgar Marchant of the *Vineyard Gazette* retorted defiantly. "We want a railroad and we are going to have it," he threatened, averring, "Refuse to encourage and lend our aid to this enterprise, and this town will disappear into the darkness of oblivion." He added, "The town will become a waste, a howling wilderness; rats and mud turtles will crawl over our streets, and owls and bats sit in our high places."

Edgartown voters supported the effort to fund the railroad, 149 to 72.

Robert Morris Copeland, the landscape architect who laid out the planned community of Cottage City, was employed to develop a similar map for the landscape in Katama, which would then serve as a basis to market house lots. However, the Panic of 1873 struck nationwide and brought ominous implications that hindered the Katama development and placed the future of the railroad in doubt.

Nevertheless, speculators won the day. By the spring of 1874, sufficient financing was in place to create a railroad line between Cottage City and Edgartown. Financing consisted of $25,000 in stock, $15,000 approved by the townspeople of Edgartown and $35,000 in town bonds. Thus, $75,000 was available to construct the line. The Martha's Vineyard Railroad was incorporated on June 17, 1874, and the train rolled along the track for the first time two months later.

Standard railroad track width was 4 feet, 8.5 inches. By using narrow-gauge track, only 3 feet wide, the operation could be completed more efficiently and cheaper. The narrow-gauge line ran a distance of nine miles, from the steamship pier in Cottage City through downtown Edgartown and on to Katama on the south shore.

The Dacey brothers of Neponset began to lay track across the island, from the Cottage City steamship pier along Beach Road, by Trapp's Pond and through the present Edgartown Golf Course to the Depot, adjacent to the House of Correction on Main Street, Edgartown. From there, the line continued through the Old West Cemetery out to Katama Bay, with an additional half-mile spur down to South Beach.

Building the track quickly was a challenge for the Dacey brothers. In May, they sent forty men to begin the project and promised another fifty would be sent shortly. But the project was not immune from labor issues. Dacey offered to pay each worker $1.75 a day. The crew wanted more money and vowed to strike if they did not receive $2.00 per day. Their wish was granted. Cost of construction for the track amounted to $94,618—$20,000 more than had been appropriated.

The entire nine miles of track, including three wyes, was completed in just sixty-six days. (The wye was a triangular junction that allowed the engine of the train to turn around by going forward, switching the track, backing up then proceeding forward again. It is comparable to a three-point turn in an automobile.)

"But the real trouble was the route itself. For the sake of expediency, half the line was laid on a beach [State Beach] that caught the worst of every northeaster that howled, and these storms buried, bent and washed away the track as if that were the weather's special project."[48] Thus, the railroad track was built on sand that shifted and drifted, eroded and washed away—an unstable surface under any circumstances.

Glacial debris on the Vineyard was not secure. The sand was unstable, which meant the track along the shoreline was wont to wiggle. It was a significant error in judgment that the railroad was built along the beach instead of the more secure inland route. The beach was formed by melting water from the glacier, like the outwash plain, similar in texture and stability to the Great Plain of the state forest in the middle of the Island.

Those who designed the route of the railroad apparently never considered the option that the track could have been located, indeed should have been located, on the inland side of Sengekontacket Pond. Admittedly, that route would have restricted the ocean view for passengers and made the overall ride a bit longer but would have eliminated numerous expenses caused by track damaged in winter storms.

Only a slight elevation was evident along the route, less than a 5 percent grade over one thousand feet, making the track relatively level and straight. In Edgartown, poles bearing warning signs were placed at marked crossings across two main roadways, presumably Main and Cooke Streets.

Three train cars were built by Jackson and Sharp in Delaware and arrived in July 1874. None was equipped with air brakes; the only brakes were on the locomotive or a cranking brake the brakeman could activate for each wheel. A link and pin assembly connected the cars. The link caused a bumpy, bouncy ride, especially when starting or stopping. Even along the relatively smooth, straight track, the ride was rough. The narrow-gauge track was lightweight, thirty pounds to a yard, yet was sufficient for the minimal rise in the route, gradual curves and weight of the train.

The Oak Bluffs was an enclosed car that seated forty-four passengers on red plush seats, four abreast. It boasted a saloon stove in the middle for passenger comfort, an ice water urn, an interior light at either end of the car and a toilet. The elaborate interior featured expansive glass windows, which added to passenger pleasure in admiring the salty scenery. There were "walk over" seats; when the train reached its destination, the conductor walked through the car, flipping the seats back to front so boarding passengers would face the direction they were headed.

A second car, the Katama, had open sides with roll-down shades against inclement weather. It seated fifty-six passengers on long wooden benches lengthwise on either side of the car. These bench seats were hard and thus less comfortable than those in the Oak Bluffs car. The Katama was trimmed out in black walnut. On a beautiful day, the sea breeze wending through the open windows was a delight.

A baggage car, known as #5, was part of this first shipment of cars. It was twenty-four feet long to accommodate luggage and freight, with seating for twenty-two additional passengers. Luggage was secured in the car and brass baggage tokens handed out to passengers to retrieve their items. The remaining brass tokens are rare reminders of the days of the Martha's Vineyard Railroad.

A third passenger car was purchased in 1876. Neither its name, number nor any identifying features or specific dimensions are known.

Brass luggage tags were issued to passengers who rode the Active. *Courtesy of Sharon Kelley, photo by Joyce Dresser.*

At a cost of $3,000, a station was built in Edgartown with track running right through it. This became the most elaborate structure of the railroad. It was not as sound as it could have been, as it sustained significant wind damage in the winter of 1876, which required major repairs.

In Oak Bluffs, a wye was placed by the Sea View House, adjacent to the current Oak Bluffs Police Station, where the engine would be turned around. A second wye was located by the Mattakeset Lodge in Katama, where the whole train would be turned around. A ticket office was located in Cottage City, along with a platform for waiting passengers by the Observation Tower along Pay Beach. Another loading platform was situated in Katama.

As for the engine, a steam dummy was first delivered to the Vineyard aboard the *Monohansett* early in August 1874. It had been built in Worcester by Wheelock and Bradley and was typical of small engines used on electric railway tracks to motor beyond where electrification ended. The engine was too slow and too weak to pull three passenger cars, and it negotiated curves poorly. The Martha's Vineyard Railroad returned the car and was refunded $2,000 after a bit of discussion.

A second engine was ordered from Porter and Bell of Pittsburgh. This was #201, thirty feet long and weighing eleven tons. It was an 0-6-0 design

The Martha's Vineyard Railroad chugged from Oak Bluffs to Edgartown along State Beach. *Courtesy of the Connie Sanborn collection.*

with six driving wheels, which meant the power was in the middle of the engine, on neither the front nor rear wheels. The engine was not specifically designed for pulling cars; however, it did the job on the Vineyard.

This engine was originally intended for the Chester and Lenoir Railroad in North Carolina, a railroad that named the little engine the Active. When the engine was redirected to the Vineyard, it was named the Edgartown, although it was known then and is still known today as the Active. Later, it was renamed South Beach.

This new first-class locomotive arrived in Woods Hole aboard a flatcar from Pittsburgh. Unfortunately, in Woods Hole, the engineer pushed the flatcar forward suddenly, and it abruptly struck a bumper on the dock. The collision caused the locomotive to fly forward, off the flatcar and right into Woods Hole Harbor, to the consternation of one and all.

Trainmen from the Old Colony Railroad line in Taunton were summoned to resurrect the engine, clean and repair it. In less than a week, the company delivered the engine aboard the *Island Home* to the wharf in South Beach near the Mattakeset Lodge. It was an auspicious start for the little engine, but the Active proved a successful form of locomotion for the residents and tourists of Martha's Vineyard, beginning in the late summer of 1874.

On August 24, 1874, the Martha's Vineyard Railroad opened for business. On its inaugural route, "gradually the engine passed the rubicon, so to speak, to the track above the Lodge, where steam was quickly made, the boilers filled, and everything prepared for the first trip of a locomotive on Martha's Vineyard."[49]

Regardless of the wariness of voters and overlooking the financial threats of the national panic, the Martha's Vineyard Railroad was heartily welcomed by the majority of Vineyarders. "Gaily decorated with flags, the engine started away at a brisk pace and rapidly made the distance toward Edgartown, producing a sensation all along the route," reported the *Vineyard Gazette*.[50]

The Active leaves the Sea View Hotel in Cottage City, bound for Edgartown. *Courtesy of Martha's Vineyard Antique Photos.*

The Active successfully towed the passenger cars from Katama to Cottage City, marking the first successful mass transit event in Vineyard history. "And at last we drew up before the 'Sea View [House],' the driving wheels ceased to rotate, and 'mid cheering, music from four bands, salutes and greetings of the most cordial description from the crowd, we alighted, and the first trip of a locomotive over the Martha's Vineyard R.R. had been successfully run."[51]

Once the train was operating in the late summer of 1874, it carried up to 150 passengers on the half-hour ride from Oak Bluffs to Katama. It operated for twenty-one full seasons, between July and September from 1875 to 1895.

Passenger traffic in the first full year of service, 1875, amounted to 28,911 fares, with the train running a total of 12,554 miles between Cottage City, through Edgartown and out to Katama. The next busiest season was 1882, when some 21,142 passengers rode the rails.

A couple of blasts on the steam whistle, the ringing of the brass bell, the build-up of steam burst from the smokestack as the fireman monitored the fire and water and the train was ready to roll. With the awkward coupling between cars, there was a jerking and lurching movement when the locomotive started and again when it slowed down and stopped.

Railroad ticket ephemera. *Courtesy of the Martha's Vineyard Museum.*

Passengers at the Martha's Vineyard Railroad Station could connect with the steamship and the Old Colony Railroad. *Courtesy of Martha's Vineyard Antique Photos.*

A round-trip ticket from Oak Bluffs to Katama cost seventy-five cents, one way was fifty cents and the spur from Edgartown to Katama was a quarter. Later, day-trippers were offered a round-trip ticket to and from Katama for a dollar that included a clambake and often a dance.

Promotions proved a positive inducement to tourists as well as locals, and special events inspired the railroad to offer extra rides out to Katama. Events hosted at the Mattakeset or the chance to see high surf at South Beach attracted more passengers. A genuine Rhode Island clambake was a popular attraction that boosted train traffic.

A popular man from the onset was conductor John Worth, according to the *Vineyard Gazette.* Worth "fills the difficult and responsible position assigned him, with a kind attention to his passengers which is rapidly warming his friends more and more along the route." In 1892, engineer Henry Luce operated the train; the conductor was Frank Hadley.

The railroad ran between twenty-five and thirty miles per hour, burning 1,500 pounds of coal per day. The route began at the steamship wharf in Cottage City, running between Ocean Park and the bathhouses on Pay Beach. Often, the train would stop at the Observation Tower by Pay Beach to pick up passengers.

The train moved along State Beach, beyond the present Bend-in-the-Road Beach and alongside Trapps Pond, thence across what is now the Edgartown Golf Course and slowed as it reached Edgartown. At the Edgartown Station, now Depot Market, the train actually ran inside the building, stopped, and passengers disembarked. Nearby was the engine house where the locomotive could be housed or repaired. From Cottage City, it took twenty minutes to reach Edgartown and another fifteen minutes on to Katama.

Passengers were excited to disembark from the railroad at the Mattakeset Lodge in Katama. *Courtesy of Martha's Vineyard Antique Photos.*

Service was reduced on Sunday because people honored the Sabbath by not riding the train to spend the day at the beach. Connections were coordinated with the steamship line, and the ferry often waited if the train was late, which was not unusual; this was greatly appreciated by tourists.

"Eventually the railroad earned a reputation as a merry and even useful thing to ride on. But it never broke even. The seasons were too short, the costs of running a train over sand from the Cottage City of America to the Nowhere of the Vineyard just too high."[52] The Martha's Vineyard Railroad was a product of the national movement of industrialization, the intent to expand from one coast to another. Although the Island railroad was a financial failure, it exemplified the can-do attitude by influential businessmen to exert their influence on the community.

The most expensive aspects of the Martha's Vineyard Railroad involved sections of railroad track that were destroyed by storms, especially along the sandy State Beach. In 1876, more than three hundred feet of track was damaged and cost $15,000 to repair. Maintenance had to be performed annually on the track. In 1879, the single trestle bridge over the entrance to Sengekontacket had to be repaired. (The second bridge, Little Bridge, was not constructed until 1937 when Sengekontacket was deemed "dirty" and a second outlet and bridge were built.)

The Active, the engine of the Martha's Vineyard Railroad, was stored and serviced in an engine house behind what is now the Dukes County House of Correction in Edgartown. Coal was housed there as well. On May 21, 1878, a fire started in oily rags in the engine house. The building was engulfed in flames when firemen arrived. They managed to haul the Active out of the flaming engine house, saving it and thus preventing a delay in summer service.

Minor accidents and incidents occurred over the years. The train struck an ox one day in Katama, and the farmer was compensated ten dollars for the injured animal. The pin and link connectors of two cars were damaged and caused a delay but no injury. In 1879, the engine pushed through a barrier and crashed into a wall of the Mattakeset Lodge, again without injury.

For one season, 1879, the engineer burned hemlock instead of coal to reduce the smoke and soot that infested the passenger cars. This was not continued thereafter, for whatever reason.

In January 1877, townspeople in Edgartown voted to withdraw from the railroad. The town lost the $15,000 it had subscribed, for a return of $315. Nevertheless, "the railroad made Edgartown a summer resort in a new sense, and for this service the town was not doing badly to have paid only fifteen thousand dollars. Over a period of years the money returned again, puffing down the narrow gauge line on the beach behind the noble Active."[53] From that point of view, the railroad was a success in enticing tourists to travel to Edgartown and on to Katama.

The Martha's Vineyard Railroad could be considered a success from the perspective that it did bring tourists out of Cottage City to enjoy South Beach and the Mattakeset Lodge. It met the needs of those people who commuted between Cottage City and Edgartown. The railroad expanded transportation opportunities for Islanders as well as connecting three very unique communities.

For all the success enjoyed by the customer base of residents and tourists, the railroad was still deemed a financial failure. Furthermore, all was not well with the premier hotels anchored at either end of the rail line. The Mattakeset Lodge and the Sea View House were individually sold in 1879, an omen of future financial failure.

Left: The Active steams by the Observation Tower along Pay Beach in Cottage City. A steamship waits at the pier. *Courtesy of Martha's Vineyard Antique Photos.*

Below: The Active returns to the Sea View Hotel in Cottage City. *Courtesy of Martha's Vineyard Antique Photos.*

Yet the little railroad continued to chug back and forth each season. On August 28, 1875, the Martha's Vineyard Railroad transported 1,800 passengers, which brought over $900 into the coffers. Over the summer of 1882, the train traveled 6,527 miles, transporting 26,142 passengers, providing Vineyarders with a reliable means of transport between Cottage

City and Edgartown, as well as Katama. Considering the hundreds of thousands of people transported across the Vineyard over twenty years, it is impressive that there is no evidence anyone was ever killed or even seriously injured during the tenure of the Martha's Vineyard Railroad. That is a safety record to be proud of.

In 1891, Old Colony Railroad assumed ownership and management of the railroad due to its financial insolvency and extensive debt.

"Sea View in Ashes" blared the headlines in the *Vineyard Gazette* of September 29, 1892. "Totally Destroyed by Fire Saturday Night." The report described a fast-moving fire, reported at 11:45 p.m., that burned the hotel, the steamship wharf, the Old Colony office, the telegraph office and the Martha's Vineyard Railroad office. Estimated loss was $80,000. The newspaper mourned the Sea View as "one of the centers of attraction to the summer visitor and our resident population." The cause was undetermined. "The whole matter is enveloped in mystery." The property of the Martha's Vineyard Railroad was not insured.

This suspicious conflagration destroyed not only the Sea View House but also part of the steamship wharf and the railroad wye, which disabled the ability to turn the engine around. Hence, for the final three years of operation, from 1893 to 1895, the Active *pulled* the train from Edgartown to Cottage City and *pushed* it, backward, from Cottage City to Edgartown. Passengers now boarded the train at the Observation Tower, which meant they had to haul their luggage from the steamship wharf the length of Ocean Park to board the train.

In 1894, service was discontinued to South Beach except for special excursions.

Track maintenance proved an ongoing issue throughout the train's tenure. In September 1895, a separated track caused a serious delay in service. That proved the death knell for the railroad; it never operated again.

The Mattakeset Lodge closed in 1905. The building was broken up in 1910, with one section removed to the Harbor View Hotel and another to the Martha's Vineyard Land Bank building across from Cannonball Park in Edgartown. Harlan Chadwick of Edgartown assumed ownership of the station platform on South Beach and transported it to the Pavilion on Chappaquiddick.

And the train itself? On May 17, 1900, the *Vineyard Gazette* reported, "Last week Friday it [Edgartown] entered the list of the few towns in the Commonwealth which has seen a locomotive traversing Main street under its own steam....Shifting sections of track were laid through the street and the locomotive went along in 3-rod runs in a very satisfactory manner."

The engine had performed admirably for twenty years, running back and forth across the Island. It had more than met its task, but times were changing, and it was time to move on. The Active locomotive was sent on to Boston to haul roadway material in East Boston and Revere. The little engine that could left the Island.

The story goes that en route to Boston, the vessel transporting the Active ran into a fog bank, and the captain of the steamer had his mate ring the Active's bell as a warning, like a foghorn—perhaps the first time a locomotive bell was heard at sea.

FINDING THE MARTHA'S VINEYARD RAILROAD

The train cars were discarded, either demolished or recycled, to resurface once again. Herman Page told an intriguing tale of the Oak Bluffs car. When he was giving a talk about the railroad, a woman in the audience called out, "There's our car!" referring to the train car.

The author [Page] was then invited to come to their home in Oak Bluffs, where he was taken down to the basement in order to look up and view what appeared to be the underside of a vintage wooden passenger car. The metal tie rods and brake rods had been removed, but all the wooden parts were there. Also, because the couple were then making renovations to their house, they had opened part of the wall in a room [the kitchen] above the car's underside. Here could be seen part of a wooden car side. The window openings were identical to those of a builder's photo of the Oak Bluffs. Further inspection of the woodwork showed traces of lettering on what had been the letter board and which consisted of "...a's Vi..." Hence, these

The remains of the luxurious Oak Bluffs railroad car became part of an Island house. *Photo by Joyce Dresser.*

traces are likely remnants of lettering on the Oak Bluffs that originally read "Martha's Vineyard Railroad."[54]

Alex Palmer and his wife purchased their house in 1995. The previous owner said she thought the remains of an old trolley car were embedded in the structure. When the Palmers had work done by a local carpenter, he pulled off some shingles and uncovered the letters *a's Vi*, which could only refer to Marth*a's Vi*neyard. He also encountered metalwork in the underside of the house that indicated metal bolts and rods, part of a train car.[55]

Alex Palmer reiterated that when Herman Page investigated the structure, he confirmed it was the luxurious enclosed Oak Bluffs train car, formerly with plush seats that now made up part of his cottage.

The structure became an essential part of the house, and the Palmers built additions around it. Alex says that when you walk about twenty-five feet into their house, the floor slopes as you exit the train car to the rest of the house.

Alex heard the rumor that another train car was buried in a ridge behind Waban Park. To his knowledge, no one has dug up or explored the area with a metal detector to try to locate another train car.

In his book *Tracing the Route of the Martha's Vineyard Railroad, 1874–1896*, Walter Blackwell followed the original route of the railroad. He documented his efforts of locating many sites along the way in July 1969 and meeting people who had uncovered remnants of the railroad, such as railroad spikes. Blackwell noted several embankments along the route and a significant cut by the Edgartown Golf Club, which served to level and straighten the train track as it approached Edgartown.

Today, one can find traces of the old railroad, just as remnants of Dr. Fisher Road are still visible. While these vestiges of the past are of most interest to historians and land conservators, there is a sense of purpose today in recognizing and admiring the diligence and desire of people from the nineteenth century to make their world a better place. They constructed roadways and railways to connect one part of Martha's Vineyard to another decades before the motorcar invaded the Vineyard. Obviously, there was a growing need to link the Island together.

For the inquisitive, remnants of the railroad line are still extant in 2017, perfectly visible in plain sight, if one knows where to look. We undertook a bit of sleuthing in autumn, when traffic and leaves are less an impediment to scrabbling about through the backwoods and roadways of Oak Bluffs and Edgartown.

We know the Active originated in Oak Bluffs, adjacent to where the current Steamship Authority pier is located. Pilings along the shore from the old railroad track are clearly visible at low tide, protruding through the sand, in line with where the track went. On this railroad trestle in Oak Bluffs, "There was nothing soon but a right of way and streak of rust, the trestlework along the beach whitened and splintered in the storms and suns of many seasons, until passersby of a new generation had forgotten why it was ever built."[56]

The track ran between Ocean Park and Pay Beach, with a stop near the juncture of Ocean and Seaview Avenues, where the Observation Tower once stood. From there, the train passed Waban/Dennis Alley Park and the Inkwell, then in front of Farm Pond. The track ran along what is now known as State Beach, adjacent to a roadway where horse-drawn wagons and people walked.

Only one bridge was built along this stretch of shoreline, meaning the water funneled in and out of Sengekontacket solely beneath what we know today as the Big Bridge. Repairs to this bridge were undertaken during

Stark pilings by the Oak Bluffs Steamship Authority pier are all that remain of the structure of the railroad track. *Photo by Joyce Dresser.*

the term of the railway, as well as annual repairs to the train track when it was damaged or destroyed by the ceaseless winds that washed ocean water against the tracks.

At the Edgartown end of State Beach, the current street turns abruptly to the right at Bend-in-the-Road Beach and meanders into town. The railroad track continued straight along the shore on the ocean side of Trapps Pond. This route extended the exposure of the railroad tracks to damage from ocean wind and water but offered an expansive view of Nantucket Sound, rarely appreciated by today's tourists.

Walter Blackwell followed the track into Edgartown from Bend-in-the-Road Beach. Beyond Trapps Pond, the train turned inland, up and into what became the Edgartown Golf Club. Today, a long, straight roadway runs parallel to the course on its eastern side, adjacent to the clubhouse. An embankment next to the dirt roadway indicates where a little hill was excavated to provide a level course for the track. The straight line of the dirt road is an obvious reincarnation of the train track. Then the track cuts into the woods behind the parking area. Standing on the private dirt road, one can clearly see the raised embankment of the track, making it level as the train was heading into town.

The Martha's Vineyard Railroad track ran alongside what became the Edgartown Golf Course. *Photo by Joyce Dresser.*

Railroad track once ran along the roadway that ran to the Long Hill Assisted Living facility, adjacent to Norton Orchard Road, Edgartown. *Photo by Joyce Dresser.*

From the Edgartown Golf Club parking area, double back to Pine Street and go left onto Norton Orchard Road. As you enter Norton Orchard, the roadway rises. Look left, to the long driveway up to Long Hill Assisted Living facility for the elderly. This is the route of the original train track.

Nosing around, I "found" this raised embankment, and it continues right by the house of Jack Blake. He was working in his yard and looked up as I passed his house. "Can I help you?" he asked. "I'm looking for the railroad," I said. "You're on it," he replied with a smile. The line ran right through his property; he parks his van on the old railroad bed. Standing on the roadway to Long Hill, the line of the railroad is clearly visible.

The train emerged from the golf course and ran directly into town, parallel to Pine Street. It was along Norton Orchard Road that young Daniel Serpa used his metal detector to find a railroad spike, a remnant of the long-lost train track. Before it reached Main Street, the engine house was located along the route to the right, behind the jail. Perhaps the concrete pediments, bearing a compass atop, denote the site of the engine house. The train emerged onto Main Street adjacent to the present-day Dukes County House of Correction. This was the site of the only actual building on the railroad, and the train steamed right into it, spewing cinders and smoke.

When the engine stopped, passengers could step off, and the train proceeded south to Katama. Today, the only reminder of the train station is the name Depot Market.

The train track crossed upper Main Street, east of Memorial (Cannonball) Park and through what today are the backyards or front lawns of prominent white clapboard, red-brick chimneyed Edgartown properties. The track crossed Cooke Street and ran directly through the Old Westside Cemetery. The route is evident; one can drive on the old railroad bed.

Crossing Robinson Road, the railroad route angled across a field, then alongside the New Westside Cemetery, behind the white fence on the east side. When I described this line to James Lengyel of the Martha's Vineyard Land Bank, he grew quite excited. "I never knew why that lot had the angle going through it, but I can see it clearly now on the topographical map." The train track was designed to run as straight and as level as possible, and the cut through the two cemeteries exemplified how and why it did.

From the New Westside Cemetery, the train headed south across Cleveland Town Road. We were able to find an area of the track bed off Mill Hill Road. Karen Zingg lives on land where one can sight the route of the train.

Depot Market sits on the site of the Edgartown railroad station. The Active would steam into the station to discharge passengers. *Photo by Joyce Dresser.*

The railroad ran along the Old Westside Cemetery in Edgartown; all that remains is a shell-covered roadway. *Photo by Joyce Dresser.*

She has found several spikes from the old railroad on her property. From there, the train ran just west of Right Fork (Herring Creek Road) before it crossed and continued on out to Katama.

More than one embankment was visible in the late 1960s when Walter Blackwell traced the route. Blackwell chatted with locals who had memories of or experiences in finding remnants of the railroad that provided him with sufficient detail to make an authoritative determination of the route of the train.

I could only imagine where the train track ran parallel to Herring Creek Road. There is no evidence of this portion of the route. Walking through the Land Bank's Norton Field, I uncovered what could have been a railroad route, as the ground was covered with crushed seashells similar to those along the cemetery route, but that is speculative. Certainly the route was nearby, though I wonder if any artifacts from it are still extant.

Walter Blackwell, in 1977, found some evidence of the train track route farther down in Katama, but I was unable to raise any indication of railroad activity. Much of the land has been plowed for farming or built up in housing developments. The Mattakeset Lodge could have been at the site of the town wharf, near the Land Bank property facing Katama Bay, Katama Point Preserve. The pier on South Beach, where the train backed up a half mile to the ocean, is long gone, and no remains are evident.

When the track reached Katama, it bore east, toward Katama Bay where the Mattakeset Lodge was located. That was the original terminus; however, another wye and a link were added so the train could back the half mile or so down to South Beach, thus affording passengers the opportunity to enjoy the ocean from the train platform. No remnants of the train track are visible in that area today, but Blackwell's research from a half century ago stands as testament to the extent of the original train service.

The challenge of locating any evidence of the Martha's Vineyard Railroad was rewarding, especially in downtown Edgartown. Other examples or evidence of the track is as much speculative as anything. In any case, there's clearly a bit of history buried in the shoreline and back lots of Martha's Vineyard, vestiges of a long-lost railroad, and well worth further exploration.

On the other side, over in Woods Hole, it is of interest to note that between 1884 and 1916, a luxury line, the Flying Dude train of the Old Colony

Line, transported the rich and famous from Boston to Woods Hole. The Flying Dude offered "privacy for the rich" in an exclusive, speedy train. This train may have borne the onus for attracting the glitterati and tycoons to Martha's Vineyard.

Once the Old Colony Line suspended rail service to Woods Hole in 1964, the track was removed and the route converted to the Shining Sea Bikeway, which opened in 1977. Today, one can bicycle many miles along the paved bike path, heading north from the Steamship Authority in Woods Hole.

Chapter 8

GETTING AROUND VINEYARD WATERS IN THE EARLY TWENTIETH CENTURY

S omehow we all made the same trolley taking us to the destination of New Bedford," wrote Frances Meikelham recalling the travails of her family's travels to reach the Vineyard in the early twentieth century.[57] The Meikelham family left their New York home and boarded the Harlem River train into New York City. There, they caught the Fall River steamer *Puritan* at Fulton Street. From Fall River, the family rode the trolley on to New Bedford and thence across Buzzards Bay on another steamer to the Vineyard.

Once on the Vineyard, the Meikelhams rented a house each summer on South Water Street until they moved to Edgartown year-round in 1916. Frances Meikelham later operated a jam and jelly shop in town, and her mother founded the Martha's Vineyard Garden Club in 1924. The Meikelhams' experience mirrors the tales of so many off-Islanders who fell for the allure of Martha's Vineyard after a delightful summer vacation.

Another tale involves a woman named Whilhelmina Lillian Chinell, affectionately known as Chiggie. Around 1900, Chiggie was bound for Nantucket for a vacation from her role as a governess. Due to choppy waters, the steamship docked at Oak Bluffs; Chiggie took the trolley out to the Alpine Hotel, in Lagoon Heights.

Chiggie never went on to Nantucket "because she loved the Vineyard, the Alpine Hotel, and her many new friends," says Nancy Noble Gardner, who knew her well. "She was bemused by the summer people who would sit in Lagoon Pond."

Chiggie assumed a grandmotherly role among locals during her summer vacations, sharing amusing stories of her life. She settled into a camp near the hotel, cooking outdoors beneath an umbrella in the rain. Chiggie built a small cottage with a summer kitchen and small dining area and vacationed there for decades. Chiggie died in 1974 at the age of 101, a Vineyarder by chance who loved the Vineyard by choice.

Lacking regular ferry service up-Island, catboats proved essential in transporting supplies from the mainland to the rural areas of Chilmark and Gay Head before adequate roadways and efficient vehicles existed. Catboats proved a popular, dependable and efficient means of transport in the waters off Menemsha and Lobsterville, up-Island in the early twentieth century.

The catboat design of a fishing boat originated in the mid-1800s and evolved into an all-purpose sailboat. It was broad of beam (wide), a single-sail gaff rig, with a centerboard. With a shallow draught, it was used to navigate sandbars and shoals along the coastline. The twenty-to-thirty-foot length made the catboat seaworthy, speedy, durable and maneuverable.

From Chilmark, fishermen sailed catboats laden with local fish across Buzzards Bay to sell them in New Bedford or Woods Hole and returned with necessities for the up-Island populace. "It is hard to realize the great extent of such shipping that was carried to Menemsha by small craft in the early 1900s."[58] Fishing up-Island was good and improved immeasurably when Menemsha Creek was dredged and the harbor expanded in 1905.

Perhaps the most common use of the catboat in Menemsha was for lobstering, although scalloping was also very productive. Under sail, the boats dragged nets for fish as well, truly a "stalwart workhorse." When a small seven-horsepower motor was applied in the early 1900s, the catboat could maneuver more expeditiously in fishing capability. And the harbor acquired another service: selling gasoline to fishermen. The last working catboat was the *Vanity*, under Captain Oscar Pease, in 1928.

In Edgartown, a Catboat Regatta was planned for Labor Day 1900, provided sufficient wind was available. The regatta was open to both locals and summer sailors. Unfortunately, due to an insufficient inducement in prizes, the race was called off. Sailboat races, however, were held in Menemsha for many years, beginning in 1910.

Another use of the popular catboat was as a party boat, where paying guests would engage the boat for a day of fishing. The *Helen*, under the aegis of Stephen Gardiner, plied the waters off Menemsha as a party boat for a quarter century, beginning in 1920.

Historian Gale Huntington defined the Nomans Land boat as unique to Martha's Vineyard. The island of Nomans Land, off Aquinnah, offered a prime fishing site in the late nineteenth century. Because no wharf or pier was built on the rugged island shoreline, innovative fishermen devised a boat that could be pulled ashore single-handedly and later launched without turning it around. The Nomans boat was double-ended, "small enough to be rowed or sailed by one man, and still roomy enough for two men, or a man and a boy, and a paying trip of fish."[59] The Martha's Vineyard Museum has a Nomans Land boat in its collection, and the Chilmark town seal boasts a Nomans boat but with two masts.

Popular fishing sites on the southwest shore of the Vineyard, Lobsterville and Dogfish Bar, were often used by men in Nomans boats. Lobsterville was a seasonal site where lobsters could be easily trapped. Dogfish Bar had a protected breakwater where catboats or Nomans Land boats could be safely and securely moored. Using the natural environment made fishing and transporting people and fish more accessible.

The late Captain Jimmy Morgan of Chilmark recalled, "For ten years I went swordfishing summers for Larsens," but not in a Nomans Land boat. His best season was when he caught more than one hundred swordfish off Nomans Land. Morgan ran a small boat off Menemsha. "There's no more swordfish off Menemsha now. Haven't been any in years," he said in a telephone interview in November 2017.

The wharf of the Steamship Authority in Vineyard Haven has been under the auspices of the authority since 1950. Steamship Authority vessels are the only ships to use that pier, "but formerly it was operated as a private enterprise," wrote Gale Huntington, "and any vessel—barge, schooner, tugboat or steamer, could lie there on payment of a wharfage fee. And very many vessels did lie there, for the harbor, for almost three hundred years, was one of the most important anchorages on the Atlantic Coast."[60]

Huntington noted that as many as one hundred sailing ships would be anchored in Vineyard Haven Harbor at one time as they awaited a favorable wind or sought supplies or repairs. By 1900, upward of two hundred ships would be crowded in the harbor, especially in stormy weather. In the Portland Gale of 1898, dozens of sailing ships were sunk or severely damaged.

Vineyard Sound was known as the busiest body of water along the Eastern Seaboard and second in the world to the English Channel. In 1845, an inventory of vessels passing the Sow and Pigs Lightship, south of Cuttyhunk, recorded 13,814 ships sailing through Vineyard Sound.

Thirty years later, in 1875, with Horatio Pease as Gay Head lighthouse keeper, the count dropped to approximately nine thousand. That reduction in the number of ships reflects larger vessels, with more cargo capacity and more motorized vessels than under sail. The opening of the Cape Cod Canal in 1914 reduced the significance of Vineyard Haven as a port of call.

Who knows what a bumboat is? With hundreds of sailing ships laden with crew lying at rest in the harbor, an opportunity arose for locals to make money selling supplies and foodstuffs to the shipboard seamen. Bumboats, often simply rowboats, circulated through the harbor, providing fresh milk, butter, eggs, vegetables and other provisions to sailors. The bumboat service was greatly appreciated. Bumboating in Holmes Hole Harbor was a profitable enterprise for the energetic entrepreneur.

A seamen's bethel is a church or religious chapel for sailors. As sailing ships dominated the oceans in the nineteenth century, the seamen's bethel became a popular service for sailors and whalers at sea for long periods of time. *Bethel* refers to a house of God. Gale Huntington described the Seamen's Bethel in Vineyard Haven as "a place where sailors from the anchored fleet could read, rest, visit with friends from other vessels, sing gospel hymns and look at the pretty girl playing the melodeon."[61]

At Tarpaulin Cove, on the Elizabeth Island of Naushon, a reading room was dedicated to providing intellectual and spiritual service to sailors restricted from their travels by ship repairs or inclement weather. Madison Edwards oversaw the Sailor's Reading Room. Between 1892 and 1912, the bethel served more than 100,000 sailors seeking solace from the weather. At times, 150 vessels were nestled in the harbor, awaiting a favorable wind or avoiding a storm.

Madison Edwards opened another reading room at Woods Hole for sailors. A missionary steamship, the *Helen May*, was consecrated in 1892 to transport sailors ashore to meet their religious and social needs. The *Helen May* was equipped with a sail to supplement its steam power. Edwards would steam out to each ship moored in Woods Hole, distributing reading material and newspapers to crews on the various vessels. In one year alone, he visited over 1,200 ships anchored in the harbor. The Bethel Society nicknamed the launch its "little devil chaser." By the turn of the century, thousands of sailors had benefited from the ministry.

On the Vineyard, "at Holmes's Wharf he [Madison Edwards] has opened a room for the use of sailors who frequent this landing. Books and papers are kept here. Not only can sailors profitably spend their time here when on shore but shipwrecked men may here obtain shelter,"[62] reported the *Vineyard Gazette*.

"The Seaman's Bethel, left corner of Water Street facing the SS ticket office, was opened in 1893 by Madison Edwards under the auspices of the Seamen's Friend Society of Boston." Edward's launch conveyed sailors from the many vessels moored in the harbor to the bethel. "Chaplain Edwards, who came here from a mission at Tarpaulin Cove, Naushon, was succeeded in 1926 by his son-in-law Austin Tower, and though the number to be served has greatly dwindled, the work is still carried on."[63]

The bethel was originally located at the present check-in shed of the Steamship Authority in Vineyard Haven, with an adjacent chapel and a museum. "The Bethel building was moved in 1995 next door to the Tisbury elementary school. It is now the home of the American Legion Hall Post 257," wrote Mark Lovewell. "The history of the society on the Vineyard is rich with lore and stories."[64]

In 1858, "a squadron of yachts of the New York Yacht Club arrived at Holmes Hole, ran around to Edgartown, and there lay at anchor while unfavorable weather kept them from sailing out to Nahant."[65] Thus began a tradition that survived well into the twentieth century and brought excitement and prosperity to both New Yorkers and Vineyarders, as well as lending its name to the main road linking Cottage City to Holmes Hole: New York Avenue.

"Each summer, plans were made for the welcoming of the New York Yacht Club, which regarded Vineyard Haven as one of the important objectives of its cruises."[66]

And the Oak Bluffs Club, founded in 1886 by Dr. Harrison Tucker, welcomed members of the New York Yacht Club to its sumptuous facility by Ocean Park in Cottage City, a trolley ride away.

It is of interest that the Norse word for headland or hill is *holl*. In the late nineteenth century, two local harbors were often spelled "Woods Holl" and "Holmes Holl." A later interpretation was that the word "hole" referred to a protected inlet or harbor. That protection was likely afforded by a nearby headland or hill.

It is curious how the sandbar in Katama Bay opens or closes depending on the wind, tides and storms. On occasion, man takes the cut into his own hands by breaking through the naturally formed sandbar. The *Vineyard Gazette* reported on March 13, 1874, "We have it from good authority that another attempt will be made to open a communication through the South Beach to the sea the coming season." When that break occurred, the water of Katama Bay became open to the ocean; over the years, it has opened and closed every so often as determined by winds and tides. As of this writing, in 2018, the cut is closed, and one can walk along Norton Point from South Beach to Chappaquiddick.

Chapter 9

EARLY AUTOMOBILES ON MARTHA'S VINEYARD

1900–1930

T he Vineyard Grove Company built an extensive boardwalk that stretched 3,500 feet along the harbor of Cottage City before Lake Anthony was opened to the ocean to form Oak Bluffs Harbor. This seaside promenade was conducive to long leisurely strolls, called "bluffing," in the late nineteenth century.

Bicycles had been invented early in the 1800s, and by the end of the century, their popularity extended across the country. Cottage City was considered the wheelman's summer paradise, according to Henry Beetle Hough of the *Vineyard Gazette*. In the late 1880s, groups and clubs of cyclists frequently visited Martha's Vineyard. "Martha's Vineyard concrete down-Island roads were said to be among the best in the nation, and were a renowned attraction for bicyclists from all over the Northeast."[67] The bicycle was the forerunner of the four-wheeled vehicle that soon proliferated on the Vineyard.

While the trolley and railroad provided admirable means of transportation, both were dependent on a metal track. Often, people had other places to go, and traveling by horse-drawn wagon or carriage, or on foot, proved treacherous, especially up-Island. In the mid-1870s, the *Vineyard Gazette* opined, "Of late years the quality of the building of new roads has agitated the people of the county."[68] The editorial concluded that current roadways should be repaired before new ones were built. "The mania for new roads, except when imperatively demanded, should be suffered to cool down."

Roadways gained import in town matters. Tisbury built a bridge over the Lagoon in 1871, but it was too weak to accommodate the weight of the trolley. Instead, the bridge inspired villagers to ride their carriages from Vineyard Haven over to Cottage City. Edgartown constructed a roadway along State Beach in 1872 and a bridge over the outlet to Sengekontacket. The road ran on sand, which washed away. In 1895, the road was rebuilt using cotton cloth, cheesecloth, to stabilize the sand rather than gravel. The cheesecloth highway succeeded.

A West Chop land development scheme, West Point Grove, was defined with a shell-covered roadway in downtown Vineyard Haven in 1888. A quarter century later, six hundred tons of crushed shells were imported to repave the route.

The concrete roadways in Oak Bluffs were in good shape. However, much of the rest of the Island was not. The majority of Vineyard roadways were rarely paved, rough, rutted routes around town, more appropriate for horse and buggy than horseless carriages.

The situation up-Island was especially poor. Roadways were narrow, steep and often with deep ruts. When an off-Island wagon driver tried to

The road from Vineyard Haven to Chilmark, 1893. "The trees are on the edge of this road and the leaves fill up the sand ruts and prevent wheels from sinking in." *Courtesy of Chris Baer. Images in public domain, archives.lib.state.ma.us/handle/2452/47883.*

navigate the roadways, he often found himself with one wheel in a rut and the other riding up on the roadside; the ruts were narrow and too deep for a conventional wagon. "Needless to say, it was no paradise for bicyclists, nor the automobiles which soon followed. In fact, it was virtually impassable for those not propelled by either hooves or feet."[69]

Over the years, and especially with the advent of the automobile, Vineyard workmen improved the roadways across the Island. The project to macadamize or pave the road from Vineyard Haven to Gay Head began in 1910 and took four years to complete. The result was a twenty-five-mile route of superb motoring for the early automobile enthusiast to drive from Vineyard Haven to Gay Head. The Edgartown–Vineyard Haven Road was paved in 1921, followed by North Road in 1929.

These newly paved roadways encouraged early touring vehicles to brave the route from down-Island out to Gay Head. An advertisement from the early 1900s promoted the idyllic way to see the Vineyard: "At the present writing, the up to date way is to take a trip in a motor car of which the Puritan is a most excellent example."[70]

"Edgartown is in the swim with the other resorts. The horseless carriage is here," the *Vineyard Gazette* cheered in late summer 1900. "The first to appear is the locomobile of Mr. Elmer J. Bliss of the Regal Shoe, who brought this vehicle down from Boston Saturday night. Mr. Bliss had his locomobile out on Sunday and it worked very satisfactorily on our streets."[71]

Later that summer, the *Vineyard Gazette* appraised the recent season, reporting, "The general verdict is that it has been a very enjoyable summer, and the season of 1900 passes into history." The reporter observed, "We miss the automobile which rushed by our door daily the past week and was taken off on the boat Monday."[72]

Joseph Chase Allen, the seminal *Vineyard Gazette* commentator, had another take on the "first car." In the late 1950s, he wrote, "The files of the old *Gazettes* will show that it is sixty years ago or more since the first so-called horseless carriage came to the Island. It was small, noisy, and painted green. Owned and driven by a man named Mulligan."

Allen expanded on this tale, interspersing tragedy in his narrative: "Somewhere in the vicinity of Tashmoo Hill, on the State Highway, a horse driven by an elderly man named Scott, was frightened by the car, and in its plunging, the driver was hurled from a load of shingles and died as a result of his injuries." Edward Mulligan, the vehicle operator, was charged with manslaughter in Ariel Scott's death, which occurred on July 19, 1902. Mulligan's trial lingered for several weeks before he was found not guilty.[73] Mulligan left the Island, and his plan to build the first golf course on the Vineyard fell into the hands of Lyman Besse, who completed the project in Oak Bluffs in 1910.

A result of this fear of future frights of horses prompted the Vineyard Haven selectmen, in 1902, to impose a speed limit of six miles an hour for automobiles driving on town roadways.

Joseph Chase Allen shared another account of early autos. He wrote of "the pure white car with vivid red leather upholstery and brass trim of William Barry Owen." Allen was fascinated by the unique style of Owen's vehicle. "These were touring cars, wide open to the weather, with right-hand drive, the emergency brake out on the running-board, and built with a tonneau [passenger seats in the back of a vehicle] almost circular, lined with seats and reached by means of a door in the center of the car."[74] Owen, it should be noted, was an executive in the Gramophone company and coined the phrase "his master's voice," based on a painting of a dog, ear cocked, listening to his master.

George Armsby's car had a single seat and was steered by a rod along the side of the car. "A 'jump-seat' opened in front of the driver, where the engine is conventionally located today. This would accommodate two persons."[75] The engine itself was neatly tucked beneath the driver's seat. Allen does not share the manufacturer of this unique vehicle, which started with a crank on the side of the car.

Allen's most captivating description of a Vineyard vehicle was that of the local physician. "The first Steamer, probably a Stanley, was owned by the late Dr. Charles F. Lane. It was a single-seated car, steered with a tiller, and the good doctor, always in a hurry, frequently left his engine running in order to avoid delay in starting, as steam pressure had to be built up before the car would move."[76]

Early automobiles were slow, cranky and loud. Like the steamships, it took time for locals to accept the new means of transport, but automobiles were here to stay.

It took longer to assert the same on Nantucket. Until 1918, Nantucket banned automobiles. Townspeople considered the horseless carriage a menace and a nuisance and thought that Nantucket could live without them. Cars were not permitted on Nantucket until the state legislature passed a bill

Horse-drawn wagons and horseless carriages converge on the wharf in Cottage City where steamer and railroad meet. *Courtesy of Martha's Vineyard Antique Photos.*

Even as the motorcar invaded the Vineyard, and eventually Nantucket, the horse and wagon continued to provide a reliable means of transport. *Courtesy of the Connie Sanborn collection.*

in 1918 that repealed the exclusion of motorized vehicles. Within a week, the New England Steamship Company transported more than two dozen cars to the Gray Lady, as Nantucket is known.

Vineyarders were not as rigid. Side-wheeler steamships regularly transported automobiles in the early 1900s, just as the ships had accommodated wagons. Cars were driven up a ramp on the side of the vessel and parked on the open deck.

In 1906, the *Vineyard Gazette* counted 175 autos on Island, although, as Arthur Railton reports in his *History of Martha's Vineyard*, "After six years of living with the motor car, the *Gazette* still saw it through the eyes of the horse."[77] There was no turning back; cars were here to stay.

An early census (1916) listed 266 automobiles registered on Martha's Vineyard. Of that number, the majority were Ford Model Ts (86), along with a number of Buicks (58), a smattering of Maxwells (25) and even a few Cadillacs (10); a variety of makes composed the remaining 87 vehicles.

Dukes County Garage had plenty of business at its Five Corners Vineyard Haven location. *Courtesy of Chris Baer, history.vineyard.net/photos.*

By 1922, the vehicle census reached 681, and there were more than 2,000 by 1936. Market data from a 1937 survey shortly after the depths of the Depression reported the Vineyard boasted 1 car for every two people. As Railton observed, "Nothing else ever had the impact of the horseless carriage. The Island would never be the same."[78]

Today, many summer residents keep a car on Island year-round or bring a second automobile in the summer. Traffic in the summer is the most hectic, with untold numbers of tourists arriving via cars transported by ferry. And some Vineyarders keep a car on the other side to eliminate steamship reservation issues. A total of 333,652 cars were transported by steamship between Woods Hole and the Vineyard in 1993. A quarter century later, in 2017, that number had expanded to 415,753, a 24 percent rise in twenty-five years. That's why there are more cars on the Island now than even a few years ago.

Will DeBettencourt of Oak Bluffs runs Binks Auto Repair, a popular garage and repair shop, operated by his father for many years. Will is constantly repairing automobiles for the local populace, but his dream is to work solely on antique autos. He showed off four vehicles retrieved from rusting refuse here on the Vineyard, cars he and his father worked on and refurbished and that are now as good as new. Will learned the love of cars from his father, who learned from his father—three generations of DeBettencourts, all devoted to the restoration of old automobiles.

1908 Model T. Will DeBettencourt rode to his wedding in this car thirty years ago. The Model T has kerosene running lights and cherry wood wheels, and the throttle is on the steering column. "It's my pride and joy," says Will.

Three pedals on the floor serve as the brake, clutch and gearshift. To put the car in reverse, the driver pumps one of the pedals on the floor. The engine has no water pump. To start the car, you need a crank. The battery sends a spark to start the engine. Headlights are gas lamps that offer a flickering flame, more to identify the car on the road than illuminate anything.

1919 Model T. George Athearn used to deliver fruit and produce around the Island in this grocery wagon. The vehicle has an electric start, not a crank, and a water pump. An added feature is a train whistle connected to

1908 Model T. Will DeBettencourt drove his daughter to her wedding in this car in 2017. *Photo by Joyce Dresser.*

1919 grocery wagon. This primitive pickup truck was once owned by George Athearn, who delivered produce on the Vineyard. *Photo by Joyce Dresser.*

1928 Model A. Will DeBettencourt and his father salvaged, refurbished and rebuilt this antique auto to be as good, or better, than new. *Photo by Joyce Dresser.*

Will DeBettencourt cruises in his 1931 Model A Roadster. *Photo by Joyce Dresser.*

the exhaust, so when driving down a hill, the driver pulls a cord and a whistle sounds, like a locomotive.

1928 Ford Model A was found in a barn on South Road, Chilmark. His father "rescued" it when Will was a boy; they had to kick the mice out when they got it. This was his father's car; his father completely rebuilt it. The car is a boxy coupe, light green, the perfect touring car.

1931 Model A Roadster. When he first got it, Will took the car apart, sandblasted the frame and sides and completely rebuilt the engine. This car has been restored from front to rear, top to bottom. The single seat is so narrow he has to drive with his arm around his wife, and she shifts. The Roadster is a deep green with yellow trim—very handsome.

Electricity arrived on Chappaquiddick in 1934, the same year the first car ferry crossed Edgartown Harbor to Chappy. Dial telephones came to Vineyard Haven in 1929, but it was not until 1955, more than a quarter century later, that the dial phone reached Chilmark and Gay Head. And Gay Head did not get on the electric grid until 1951; the Gay Head lighthouse was the last in the United States to be electrified.

When Elmer Bliss first drove his steam-powered Locomobile through the streets of Edgartown in 1900, he could not have imagined how rapidly and dramatically the automobile would impact the Island.

The first automobile dealership opened in the summer of 1903, when a businessman from New Bedford set up a "stable" for horseless carriages in Cottage City. This entrepreneur offered to sell and store automobiles and sell carriages.

It took a few years for Vineyarders to acknowledge the opportunities and advantages of automobiles on the Island. The *Martha's Vineyard Herald* even suggested a flagman should walk ahead of an automobile, warning of its impending arrival.

Automobile dealerships maintained reliable local service over the years, based on advertisements in the *Martha's Vineyard Guide*, published in the 1950s and '60s by the chamber of commerce:

> *1953: Bergeron Garage in Oak Bluffs sold Nash; Dukes County Garage in Vineyard Haven sold Chevy; Renear's Garage, also in Vineyard Haven, sold Ford.*
> *1956: Leonard's Garage in Oak Bluffs sold Hudson.*
> *1960: Old Colony in Edgartown sold Willys and Chrysler-Plymouth; Renear's still sold Ford.*

In 2018, the only automobile dealer on Island was McCurdy Motorcars in Vineyard Haven, selling used vehicles. On the Vineyard, many cars change hands through classified advertisements or for-sale signs in the windows, or simply word of mouth. And options to purchase a new car off-Island or online are myriad.

Chapter 10

FERRY SERVICE

1900-1924

One thing is certain about steamship service: it is an expected commodity for Islanders, especially as more and more people travel greater distances to reach the Vineyard. As the Steamship Authority booklet reminisces, "The ferries have always been the Island's lifeline, and their particularities stay with us—in historical documents, in photographs, and in our memories—even after the boats sail away for good."[79]

A notice promoted by the New Bedford, Martha's Vineyard and Nantucket Steamboat Company advertised service for the approaching summer that included daily service from New Bedford to Nantucket yet stopped at Woods Hole, Vineyard Haven and Cottage City, as well as Edgartown, en route. The steamship met trains in New Bedford from Boston, Providence, Taunton and Fall River. An extensive network of ferry service evolved by the end of the nineteenth century, prior to the arrival of the automobile.

A brief news note in the *Vineyard Gazette* at the turn of the century observed, "A large number from here took the excursion steamer *Martha's Vineyard* this morning, at 9:15, on an excursion to Nantucket. The steamer already had on board a large number of excursionists from Falmouth Heights and Cottage City."[80]

In 1902, the *Uncatena* (1902–28) went into service, weighing 652 tons and 187 feet long. Its bow deck was open to accommodate freight, the last steamship so equipped, and it was also the last side-wheeler to service the Vineyard. The *Uncatena* was the first steamboat built with a steel hull rather than a wooden frame. The *Uncatena* ran primarily between Edgartown and

New Bedford. Uncatena is the name of one of the Elizabeth Islands, the one closest to Woods Hole.

"Without any sacrifice of passenger comforts, she could carry much more freight than the larger *Gay Head*, having a twelve foot hold depth," noted the steamship company.[81] Services included a glassed smoking cabin, entered from the outside deck, and a sign that read, "No smoking abaft the shaft," which meant smoking was forbidden to the rear of the paddlewheel axle.

The *Uncatena* was the first Vineyard steamboat equipped with battery-operated electric lights. And for night trips, the *Uncatena* featured a searchlight to scan the waters ahead. Once the steamship company realized the advantages of electric lights, the rest of the illumination on the fleet was converted from oil to electricity.

For many years, Captain Marshall, a strict disciplinarian, was in charge of the *Uncatena*. During a labor strike, when the crew refused to disembark, it was said Captain Marshall had the recalcitrants tossed over the gangplank.

In 1925, the *Uncatena* ran aground near the shore of New Bedford Harbor, adjacent to the railroad line. With the power of a local locomotive, the *Uncatena* was pulled back into the harbor, the first steamship towed by a railroad engine.

After more than a quarter century of steaming back and forth across Vineyard Sound, the *Uncatena* was removed from service in 1928, sold and renamed the *Pemberton*. Its waning years were engaged on excursions out of Boston, along the North Shore to Nantasket Beach. Eventually, this rugged, faithful steamship was broken up and sold for scrap in 1937.

The *Sankaty* (1911–24) was the first propeller-driven steamer in Vineyard service. On its maiden run from New Bedford to Nantucket, "she swung into Woods Hole, Vineyard Haven and Oak Bluffs, but didn't stop. She just wanted to give everyone in the area a chance to see what she looked like."[82]

This steamship moved by a propeller rather than a paddlewheel, had two smokestacks and was heated by steam. The *Sankaty* boasted an enclosed bow, utilized for freight. With sufficient deck space, the *Sankaty* could accommodate up to six automobiles driven up on planks placed alongside the vessel.

During this era, the *Sankaty* made the fastest steamship run across Buzzards Bay in 1913. The *Sankaty* left Nantucket at 1:45 p.m. and reached New Bedford at 5:04 p.m., a travel time of three hours and nineteen minutes. That record still stands more than a century later.

Other incidents involving the *Sankaty* were not so praiseworthy.

"The *Sankaty* got herself into trouble" on February 20, 1917. First, the steamship encountered fog, en route from Edgartown to New Bedford.

The paddle-wheeler *Uncatena* operated on Vineyard Sound from 1902 to 1928. *Courtesy of Chris Baer, history.vineyard.net/photos.*

On the approach to the harbor, still in Buzzard's Bay, the *Sankaty* ran onto rocks "and was badly holed by the accident."[83] Repairs were not completed until March 30, more than a month after the incident. The next year, the *Sankaty* was trapped by ice in Nantucket Harbor from January 29 to February 13, 1918.

A nor'easter hit the Vineyard hard in October 1923. The *Vineyard Gazette* shared the drama of the day: "The waves dashed wildly over the jetties on two or three days and it was a surprise to many that on Tuesday, the wildest of the wild days, both the *Sankaty* and the *Islander* made their trips." The news report continued: "One gentlemen was almost sure that the waves dashed into the smokestack once or twice when the boat was rocking its liveliest."[84]

A serious situation occurred the next year. Hay bales aboard the *Sankaty* caught fire in New Bedford Harbor in 1924. The hay caused nearby barrels of oil to burst into flame, and soon the ship was afire. The *Sankaty* was cut free from its mooring and drifted out and across the harbor. Below deck, the captain and crew awoke, were unable to put out the flames and jumped overboard.

The *Sankaty* drifted against the whaleship *Charles W. Morgan*, which caught fire. Fortunately, the Fairhaven Fire Department successfully saved the historic whaleship and spent most of the night working to contain and extinguish the flames. They saved the *Charles W. Morgan*, but the *Sankaty* sank.

Two months later, the *Sankaty* was hauled out, sold and rebuilt, and it worked for years as a car ferry in Long Island Sound. Prior to World War II, the *Sankaty* was sold to a Nova Scotia company, converted to a minesweeper by the Canadian government and served in the war. Until 1964, the *Sankaty* still plied the waters off Prince Edward Island.

Following the sinking of the *Sankaty* in 1924, a new steamer was purchased to provide service for the islands. The *Myles Standish*, an old paddle-wheeler, operated that summer until it grounded on a rock between Vineyard Haven and Oak Bluffs. The paddle-wheeler *South Shore* was put into service to fill the gap.

A small steamer, the *Frances*, was also used to run two round trips a day from Vineyard Haven to Woods Hole in the late 1920s. Being a Vineyard man, Captain Manny Sylvia appreciated serving at the helm of the *Frances*, as he could bunk in his own home at night. However, Vineyarders did not appreciate the *Frances*, considering the vessel too small and the service inadequate.

The New York, New Haven and Hartford Railroad Company took control of the steamship company in 1911, forming the New England Steamship Company.

Due to increased costs associated with running regular service to the Islands and a decrease in passenger and freight travel, the steamship company, operated by the railroad, paid little attention to the wants and needs of Islanders. To cut costs, it reduced the number of trips during the winter in the early 1920s. The wharf in Edgartown was deactivated as a steamship landing. Oak Bluffs and Vineyard Haven provided docking services for automobiles, freight and passengers.

When the New Haven Railroad Company was compelled to sell its interest in the steamship line, the New England Steamship Company assumed management of the Island steamers. The steamships were deemed in bad shape, in need of repair, refurbishment or replacement.

Chapter 11

AIRPLANES ON THE VINEYARD

1919–1940

After nearly a quarter century, electric trolley service ended on Martha's Vineyard. Competition from automobiles and the opportunities afforded by jitney service contributed to the decline of the trolley. Nevertheless, horse and electric trolley service had operated on the Vineyard from 1873 to 1918, forty-five years.

During World War I, the government put out a call for as much iron as possible for use in munitions and military equipment. As soon as the trolley system closed down, the iron rails of the track were retrieved and sent off to the federal government.

On Tuesday, July 15, 1919, the first hydroplane, a Curtiss Seagull, landed in Oak Bluffs Harbor. Actually, it was a pair of planes from the Chatham Naval Air Base visiting the Vineyard to promote the promise of air travel.

In a descriptive account akin to a visit from outer space, the *Vineyard News*, a short-lived local newspaper, reported, "A great crowd gathered Tuesday afternoon on the beach about the wharf when two hydroplanes from Chatham alighted in the water and one came to the wharf, the other to the shore. After staying for about an hour and a half, they returned to Chatham." Air transport had arrived.

"Weekly Trips to Island by Airship" blared a headline in the *Vineyard Gazette* the following week. The article noted, "The first aerial commuters in New England are to land here Friday evening." Melvin Fuller and Myron Brown were successful New York stockbrokers with summer homes in Oak Bluffs. The two men intended to "try the flight, it was learned today, with a view to establishing this means of travel as a week-end event to and from their offices and summer houses."[85]

Details of the impending flight continued: "The plane—a Curtiss flying boat of the latest type—will be piloted by Lieutenant David McCulloch." Enthusiasm was contagious. "The coming of the commuters by air has excited this island and its hundreds of summer residents and vacationists as never before." The plan was to anchor the hydroplane in the harbor and offer flights to interested participants. Fuller added to the drama: "The Curtiss people tell us the flight can be made in a bit more than three hours."

A week later, the headline in the *Vineyard Gazette* read, "New York to Vineyard Sea Plane Arrives Friday." The newspaper referred to the "wealthy New York stockbrokers" and credited them with planning to establish "a new means of community over the weekend when they arrive Friday evening aboard a flying boat."[86]

The *Gazette* article was rhapsodic: "As the seaplane crept into the harbor, escorted by a powerboat that had been sent out to meet it, hundreds on the shore of the island cheered and waved handkerchiefs. It was a new era introduced to the summer colonists."

Fuller stated that a quarter century ago it had taken him four days to sail up from New York to the Vineyard. On July 25, 1919, they completed the flight in two hours and thirty-five minutes, compared to a long day by train and steamer. Fuller described the flight: "The first part of the trip was rough, the air being rather bumpy and full of air pockets." Pilot Griffin took them up to one thousand feet, then down to four hundred feet, "where we found the air very smooth and traveling most enjoyable." The so-called Fuller Flyer had an open cockpit, and the pilot was seated behind the two passengers.

Because it was a hydroplane, the Fuller Flyer took off and landed in Oak Bluffs Harbor, tying up at the pier of the Wesley House, to the delight of locals, guests and tourists. In an effort to promote flying, Fuller invited paying customers to take a turn aloft. Seventy-four people paid ten dollars each for a ride, including ten-year-old Margaret White, the youngest passenger. Other than a couple of minor mishaps when a pontoon or two were punctured and quickly repaired, the weekend proved a success.

An early passenger plane lands in Vineyard Haven Harbor. *Courtesy of Chris Baer, history.vineyard.net/photos.*

Eugene O'Neill, one of the more prominent playwrights of the twentieth century, reported for the *Vineyard News* on July 31, 1919: "It was a period of intense interest and enjoyment for those who made ascents." A later writer observed, "Surely O'Neill was the most talented writer ever to report the news for a Vineyard newspaper although the article provides little evidence of his future greatness."[87]

Eugene O'Neill organized a banquet at the Wesley House, followed by a public reception that filled the Tabernacle. Oak Bluffs knew how to celebrate this momentous event.

On July 29, a third airplane landing occurred, this time from the New England Airplane Company located in Hull, south of Boston. The *Gazette* reported the hydroplane, the Sea Gull, "made many flights from the Edgartown Bathing Beach, carrying pairs of passengers aloft." The article continued that "the plane sailed through the air as gracefully as a bird at an average altitude of about 500 feet." It concluded, "Looks like a bird soaring above us and yet when down in the water it looks so simple. What would the people of the next generation think of the sight?"[88] Even a century later, the miracle of air travel impresses.

In 1925, the Katama Airfield opened on the wide coastal plain of south Edgartown. The Katama heathlands were an ideal grassy field for an airport.

Within two years, airplanes were delivering daily newspapers, meeting requested trips to Boston and charters to New York City.

An airplane meet was held in 1928 with nearly two dozen planes competing in aeronautic aerobics. Ten thousand spectators appreciated parachute jumps and plane races around the Island's water towers. Ninety-one-year-old Sarah Vincent enjoyed her first flight; she had no fear of flying and considered it a "ride of a lifetime."

The Curtiss Summer Flying School was introduced at the Katama Airfield in 1929, and students began to earn their wings aloft.

Nantucket's *Inquirer Mirror* issued a contrarian report that denied there was an airport on the Vineyard and stated that planes would likely no longer land there. The *Vineyard Gazette* was vehement in its retort, with the headline "Cape Stop Will Be Used Should Nantucket Sink or Drift Away." Henry Beetle Hough penned an editorial laden with sarcasm:

> *For lo, these many years, Nantucket has boasted of its whaleships, which sailed from Edgartown and Vineyard Haven, and of its famous seafarers, who for the most part were born on the Vineyard. It surprised no one, therefore, to read in the Nantucket newspaper that the Vineyard has no flying field and that planes would probably no longer stop on the island.*

By 1938, the Martha's Vineyard Flying Club was organized, and Katama continued to serve as one of "the best natural flying fields outside of the state of Texas."[89] The popularity of flying drew dozens of pilots to Katama; more than one hundred planes a month were landing there in the late 1930s.

Steve Gentle, an avid local pilot, claimed several famous airmen visited Katama Airfield. He named daredevil aviator Rosco Turner, premier pilot, and reclusive Howard Hughes and believed he had evidence that Charles Lindbergh made it to Katama with his *Spirit of St. Louis*. Lindbergh, of course, had flown from New York to Paris in 1927, the first transatlantic air flight. Gentle had seen a photograph with Charles Lindbergh. (Lindbergh spent more time on the Vineyard during the war, so he may have visited the Vineyard earlier.)

Like all coastal airports, Katama Airfield was closed to the public during World War II and used only by the Civil Air Patrol and the National Guard.

In 1944, Gentle purchased the airfield. The Great Atlantic Hurricane of September 1944 decimated the tin hangar in Katama. Gentle rebuilt the hangar and painted the roof with the word *Katama*, visible even in the fog. Gentle operated the Katama Airpark until 1985.

The first airfield at Katama, late 1920s. *Courtesy of Chris Baer, history.vineyard.net/photos.*

Prior to the end of World War II, a new airline company, Trans Marine Airlines, advertised service between New York and the Vineyard, Nantucket and Cape Cod. Postwar promotions were underway.

After the war, in 1946, the Katama Airpark expanded its territory. In notes collected by owner Steve Gentile, he describes the purchase of twenty acres of additional land and a building that was moved adjacent to the airfield. This was the home of the great-grandparents of Daniel Serpa, and the building was later converted to the popular Right Fork Diner.

Katama is the largest grass airport in the United States, with three runways; the longest runway is four thousand feet. However, there are no nighttime takeoffs or landings.

In 1950, the Martha's Vineyard Air Seamen came to Katama for flight school. Over the years, those pilots who learned to fly at Katama have had the honor of having their shirttails on display from the rafters of the Right Fork Diner.

One fatality occurred at the airpark in 1975. War Bird pilots, veterans of World War II, visited the Vineyard in a dozen vintage planes. An aerobatic pilot attempted a roll and failed; his plane crashed, killing him instantly. It was the only fatality in fifty years.

In the 1980s, The Nature Conservancy (TNC) became involved in protection of the natural habitat on Katama. According to Brendan O'Neill of the Vineyard Conservation Society, the Katama Airfield encompasses a "unique sand-plain grassland habitat, important to more than a dozen rare plant and animal species. Ecologists referred to the Katama habitat as 'something of a living museum; a kind of Galapagos.'" That made it essential to preserve and protect the site by restricting development and protecting the natural wildlife habitat. According to O'Neill, "In the public eye, the initiative became a 'Race to Save the Coastal Heathlands.'"[90]

The Nature Conservancy joined the Vineyard Conservation Society in 1983 to purchase the airpark from the Gentle family and presented it to Edgartown in 1985. In return, Edgartown provided TNC with a conservation restriction on the property. The airpark was preserved and development restricted. The Katama Airfield survives in the midst of a protected grassy plain.

Another more major airport was built in 1942 when the U.S. Navy appropriated a square mile of the state forest to construct the Martha's Vineyard Airport in the middle of the Island. It was used in World War II initially to launch planes to protect convoys heading to Europe from U-boats, or German submarines. Later, the airport became a training site for pilots dispatched to the Pacific theater.

In 1946, the military moved out and commercial flights were established. Northeast Airlines booked flights to New York and Boston. In 1969, an effort was made to extend the runways on the Martha's Vineyard Airport to accommodate jet planes. This necessitated appropriating another square mile of the state forest and repairing the Edgartown–West Tisbury Road, removing a glacial mound that prompted a sarcastic campaign to "Save the Sub-Standard Bump," a slight rise in the road where speeding teenagers could momentarily go airborne.

The first commercial jet landed on the Vineyard in 1970. President Bill Clinton arrived aboard Air Force One during his seven Vineyard vacations in the 1990s.

Today, Cape Air meets the needs of residents of the Vineyard and Nantucket with connections to Hyannis and Boston in small eight-seated planes, perfect to accommodate local traffic.

Chapter 12

STEAMSHIPS

1925–1950

Anew set of priorities was laid out by the New England Steamship Company in the 1920s. It was determined to rebuild its fleet of steamships, and the result became known as the White Fleet: four new steamships, all white, built to serve the Islands.

The first steamship was the *Islander* (1923–56). Three other ships followed: the *Nobska*, the *New Bedford* and the *Naushon*. "For their time, the steamers of the White Fleet were probably the most successful, recognizable, and popular of any to service the islands of Martha's Vineyard and Nantucket. If any vessels can be said to be symbolic of boats to the islands, it is these four."[91]

The *Islander*, built by Bath Iron Works in Bath, Maine, was the first completely steel-hulled steamship in Vineyard service. The vessel was propeller driven, with a saloon and hurricane decks, and could accommodate twenty-five cars. "She was the prototype for the island steamers of the 1920's and her smooth, clean lines and straight, pointed bow and bellied-out mid section made her class of vessel one of the most attractive in appearance of all the ships to have been in island service."[92]

The interior of the vessel matched its impressive exterior.

> *In the lobby were rolled, wood-slatted, stationary benches on either side, with Windsor chairs placed in the center. At the base of the stanchions, brass cuspidors (a spittoon, for chewing tobacco) were conveniently located. A wide stairway led from the lobby to the saloon above. The base of the stairway was flanked to port by the men's room and to starboard by the smoking and card room.*[93]

Writing desks equipped with stationery were provided, as well as pens and ink. Staterooms could be rented to assure privacy on the route across the waters.

In 1928, the *Islander* was renamed the *Martha's Vineyard*.

Initially, the White Fleet burned coal to build steam. In 1934, all four steamers were converted to oil, a more efficient and less expensive fuel. Years later, diesel became the fuel of choice. Also that year, the Vineyard ports for the steamship were altered: "Edgartown was once the major port on the Vineyard and was the primary destination for steamboats. Eventually, these two harbors, Oak Bluffs and Vineyard Haven, gained most of the traffic, and the last steamer out of Edgartown was the *New Bedford* on November 9, 1934."[94]

After more than thirty years of reliable service plying the waters of Vineyard Sound, the *Islander/Martha's Vineyard* was sold to a Rhode Island firm and converted from steam to diesel. It was put in service between Hyannis and Nantucket from 1962 through 1966 and later worked Long Island Sound. In 1970, passengers viewed the America's Cup races from the deck of the *Islander/Martha's Vineyard*.

An effort to outfit and finance the vessel to offer dinner cruises never came to fruition. The *Martha's Vineyard* was docked at Charlestown Navy Yard, where it met an ignoble end, sinking in 1990. Once raised, it was sold for scrap. The *Martha's Vineyard* lives on, symbolically, in the logo of the current Woods Hole, Martha's Vineyard and Nantucket Steamship Authority.

The *Nobska* (1925–73) was the second steamship in the White Fleet, named for the spit of land adjacent to Woods Hole, adorned with a lighthouse. The *Nobska* was also built at Bath Iron Works, nearly identical to its sister ship the *Martha's Vineyard*. (One difference was that the space between the pilothouse windows was narrower in the *Nobska*, for improved visibility.)

The *Nobska* was 210 feet long and ran on a 1,200-horsepower engine, steam-powered and fueled originally by coal, later converted to oil and still later to diesel. The *Nobska* could accommodate 1,200 passengers and moved at fourteen knots. Automobiles were loaded from the side of the ship, which was slower than entering from the stern. A unique form of communication in this era was that two voice tubes were used, one to communicate between the captain in the pilothouse and the mate on the freight deck and a second voice tube linking the captain to the engineer in the engine room.

The *Nobska* was initially under the command of Captain James Sandsbury. Captain Manuel Sylvia was in charge of the *Islander*.

A weather vane of the steamship *Nobska* sits atop the Oak Bluffs steamship building. *Photo by Joyce Dresser.*

In 1928, the *Nobska* was renamed the *Nantucket*; however, it was still known as the *Nobska* by its faithful patrons. As noted, that same year, the *Islander* was renamed the *Martha's Vineyard*.

A memorable incident occurred with a runaway cart on the freight deck of the *Nobska/Nantucket*. Apparently, the vessel was on a rough ride, and a freight cart laden with a tombstone rolled back and forth, spooking the crew.

Often the steamers delivered mail and newspapers to the crew aboard lightships in Vineyard Sound. This service was terminated by the Coast Guard in 1936 yet had been in practice for many years.

The *Nobska/Nantucket* "made the roughest island passage of the century on December 27, 1930." Leaving the Oak Bluffs pier at 1:30 p.m., the steamship weathered dense fog, strong winds, heavy rain and very high seas that rocked the ship, requiring that "many passengers lay down on the carpeted decks."[95] It was after dark before the ship reached Nantucket, and many passengers confirmed it was a frightening experience.

Between 1933 and 1936, when steamship business slowed due to the Depression, the *Nobska/Nantucket* was taken out of service to the Islands and relegated to running excursions from Providence to Oak Bluffs, providing access to the Vineyard for those people who lived in southern New England.

Another fond *Nobska* memory was that Charles Lindbergh used to don a disguise to avoid fellow passengers. (He lived on the Vineyard for a period of time during the war to keep a low profile after being admonished in the press for his isolationist and "America first" statements. Later, Lindbergh had a change of heart and joined the U.S. Army Air Forces.) Once, his wife, Anne Morrow, couldn't find the famous aviator. He was secluded below deck, out of sight, dining with the crew.

The *Nobska* proved an excellent steamship in the ice, especially for Nantucket runs. However, it was stuck in ice off Nantucket for a month in the winter of 1961. The *Nobska* was frozen in place; once the ice broke up, the ship was freed once more.

Of the four vessels in the White Fleet, the *Nobska* was the last one still in service to the Vineyard; its final run was in 1973, just short of a half century of service.

The *New Bedford* (1928–42) was slightly larger than the other ships of the White Line and thus could accommodate more vehicles. Its design was similar to its predecessors', although an effort was made to make more space for freight.

On its maiden voyage, the *New Bedford* passed the aging *Uncatena*. "As the old passed the new and the *Uncatena* saluted her successor, there was a mingling of sentiments felt by those on board for the handsome, new arrival."[96] Captain Marshall was at the helm when the new *New Bedford* was launched and steamed from its namesake city to Oak Bluffs and on to Nantucket. The *New Bedford* was "glistening with new paint and riding the dull gray sea easily and smoothly."[97]

Carrying more automobiles was the intention, but loading the cars was not easy. Automobiles were driven onto the *New Bedford* through the side of the ship and then had to turn sharply to maneuver up a sloping gangplank onto the vessel.

In 1934, the *New Bedford* was heading in to Woods Hole from Providence. The ship ran aground on a rocky outcropping of Uncatena Island in the Elizabeth Islands chain. The captain managed to maneuver the vessel into shallow water, and the ship was temporarily repaired before a complete fix in Boston.

On August 4, 1942, the steamship *New Bedford* was called into national service in the war effort, and it never returned to the Vineyard. For the duration of World War II, the *New Bedford* worked in the British navy, going back and forth across the English Channel, transporting troops and supplies to the Allied effort in Normandy, working in tandem with the *Naushon*. The

The *Naushon* (1929–42) was considered the Queen of the Island Fleet. *Courtesy of Chris Baer, history.vineyard.net/photos.*

two Vineyard steamships served as troop carriers as well as hospital ships from the Normandy invasion though the end of the war.

Afterward, the *New Bedford* was put on a summer line in Rhode Island between Providence, Newport and Block Island. It was last seen in a junkyard on Staten Island in 2009.

The *Naushon* (1929–42), Queen of the Island Fleet, was the last, largest and longest of the White Fleet at 250 feet. The twin screw propeller was more than sufficient to cross Vineyard Sound. Its name came from another Elizabeth island.

The *Naushon* boasted thirty-two staterooms, each with hot and cold running water and some with their own toilets. When a patron requested a stateroom, he or she was handed a four-inch-long key to open the door. A large glass observatory was situated near the stern of the vessel. Writing desks were supplied with monogrammed stationery. The *Naushon* evoked a royal steamship.

On its maiden voyage, several prominent Vineyarders were aboard, among them Stephen Carey Luce, the banker and politician; George Fred Tilton, the whaleman; and Joseph Chase Allen, the newspaperman.

The *Naushon* was the last vessel commissioned and built by the New England Steamship Company. Four new steamships had been built and launched within seven years. The White Fleet exemplified a unity of design and uniformity of equipment, unique in the history of Vineyard steamships. During the 1920s, additionally, the company rebuilt the wharves in Oak Bluffs, Nantucket, New Bedford and Woods Hole.

During the summer of 1929, so many cars had been brought to the Vineyard that an extra ferry was added for a month to return vehicles back to the mainland. The *Frank E. Gannett* was a double-ender, a true ferry, and dutifully transported the autos of the summer people back to the mainland.

In an effort to cut costs and minimize repairs, in 1930, the ships in the White Fleet were painted gray to cover aging rust spots. Public outrage was swift and severe, so the steamship company made the needed repairs and quickly repainted the vessels a bright white.

An incident occurred in 1931 when the *Naushon* collided with the schooner *Alice S. Wentworth* in Vineyard Haven Harbor. The *Naushon* was about to dock in heavy winds when a U.S. Coast Guard boat cut in front. As the *Naushon* sought to avoid collision, it was blown into the sailing ship and ran aground in the harbor. Several other boats broke from their moorings and collided with the *Naushon* as well.

The next year, 1932, the *Martha's Vineyard/Islander*, under Captain Charles Leighton, was caught in a fog bank off Nantucket. Captain Leighton proceeded cautiously, blowing his foghorn, but the sound was distorted. He followed protocol, moving slowly and sounding his horn.

At the same time, the steamship *Nantucket/Nobska* was proceeding in the opposite direction. Captain James Sandsbury, the veteran steamship captain, was at the helm. Both vessels were "completely enveloped by the fog."

Suddenly, the bow of the *Nantucket* materialized out of the fog. The *Nantucket* smashed into the port of the *Martha's Vineyard* before either captain could avert the crash. Two hundred frantic frightened passengers were aboard the steamers; only one suffered a minor injury.

The two wounded steamboats limped in to Oak Bluffs. Neither vessel was seriously damaged, but passengers and crew were shaken. The incident was attributed to the dense fog and uncertain movements of the tide and swells. The accident was deemed unavoidable, with no blame assigned.

Both Charles Leighton and James Sandsbury had served as responsible, reputable steamship captains for many years and continued working together another fifteen years. "A trial was held, but no guilt was found, as both captains followed proper procedures. They went on to work together for many years."[98]

An immediate consequence of this collision was the installation of wireless ship-to-shore communication on all the steamships. Safety cannot be minimized.

The *Naushon* once ran aground in Vineyard Haven Harbor in 1935, again under Captain Sandsbury, but was undamaged. Any collision or grounding was cause for concern, but again, no assignment of blame was made.

Islanders depend on steamship service and expect it to continue as a reliable part of their lives. Complaints and occasional delays or cancelled service are part of steamship service, due to the whims of weather and mechanical incidents. Overall, steamship service through the 1930s was commendable. Businesses depended on the steamship company to transport tourists from the mainland and to deliver goods to meet the needs of both tourists and locals, year-round, and this was the way it worked.

Zadoc Cottle of West Tisbury was a fisherman, a whaleman and a mate aboard three-masted schooners. And he was a key employee in the 1930s when he served as the engineer who ensured the steamship ran smoothly. At different times, Cottle worked as the engineer aboard the *Sankaty*, the *Nobska* and the *Martha's Vineyard*.

Rumblings of labor unrest bubbled forth in the spring and early summer of 1937. A three-day strike by steamship employees in April threatened transporting supplies to Vineyard businesses. That work stoppage expanded into a two-week strike before it was mediated, which resulted in higher pay and better working conditions for steamship employees yet had no impact on the Vineyard summer season.

Months after the United States entered World War II, the War Shipping Administration appropriated the *Naushon* on July 9, 1942. The *Naushon* was assigned to serve overseas and became Hospital Ship #49 under British command. Steel plates were attached to enclose the open decks, and the ship was painted battleship gray. With the *New Bedford* and six other steamships, a convoy known as the Honeymoon Fleet proceeded gingerly across the Atlantic, guarded by two destroyers. Off Ireland, U-boats sank three of the steamships, but the *Naushon*, *New Bedford* and three others reached Scotland. Fortunately, there was no loss of life in the crossing.

The *Naushon* participated in the siege at Normandy and transported the first casualties back to England. Jimmy Morgan of Chilmark, who served in World War II, felt the pangs of homesickness when he saw the HMS *Naushon* at a pier in Cherbourg, France. "I was on a Liberty ship," he recalled. "She had a red cross painted on her; white with a red cross. She was a hospital ship." How did he recognize the ship? "I knew it was her right off, from her profile. We knew all the steamers in those days, the *Martha's Vineyard*, the *Nantucket*."[99] Of the *Naushon*, Morgan said, "She was more elaborate." Imagine being on the other side of the Atlantic and catching sight of a familiar ferry in the midst of the war.

Both steamships were used as troop carriers and hospital ships. The *New Bedford* was an active participant at Omaha Beach on D-day. More than forty thousand troops were transported across the English Channel aboard these steamers.

Following service overseas, neither steamship returned to the Vineyard. The *Naushon* was renamed the *John A. Meseck* and refitted as an excursion vessel out of Rye, New York. The *Meseck* plied the Hudson River up to Bear Mountain for many years. It was scrapped in 1974.

The *New Bedford* was likewise refitted and served Block Island and Providence, Rhode Island. The *New Bedford* ended its days in the salvage yard on Staten Island in 1969.

During World War II, only the *Martha's Vineyard* (formerly the *Islander*) and the *Nantucket* (formerly the *Nobska*) provided regular, though limited, service to the Islands. Both vessels were painted gray to disguise their purpose. Aboard ship, lights were dimmed and cameras forbidden. Boat schedules were not printed to make steamship travel a challenge for any German spies.

After the war, in 1946, the *Hackensack*, an automobile ferry, was purchased to meet increased demand. The engine was converted from coal to oil. Ramps for cars were constructed in Vineyard Haven and Woods Hole to accommodate automobiles.

The *Hackensack* was already forty years old when it began service to the Vineyard, yet it was a double-ender, a real ferry. The *Vineyard Gazette* opined, "A glance at her ponderous lines will show why your true islanders deeply resent a reference to the trim steamboats which serve the Vineyard and Nantucket, as ferries." The *Hackensack* was renamed the *Islander* and "proved that a double-ended ferry operation on a shuttle basis, was indeed practical. Whether appreciated or not, the *Hack* pioneered the way for the more efficient and convenient type of service that is now available to modern travelers."[100]

One day in December 1947, business was so slow that the *Nantucket* steamed to the mainland with no freight, no cars and not a single passenger. True, it was early winter and business was slow, but an empty vessel had never happened before.

Stockholders of the New England Steamship Company sold out to the Massachusetts Steamship Company in 1945. Another labor disruption occurred the next year, causing a service delay. Mail was flown in for three days until the strike was settled. Poor service, financial floundering and labor strikes led politicians to the realization that ferry service to the Islands was essential and must become a state-run operation.

Once again, the New Haven Railroad assumed control of steamship service, which evolved into the Massachusetts Steamship Line. At that point, because it was clear Vineyarders relied on steamship service, a state-run organization took over the route.

In 1949, the Massachusetts state legislature authorized and created the New Bedford, Woods Hole, Martha's Vineyard and Nantucket Steamship Authority. Stephen Carey Luce was named the Vineyard representative. Today, the authority is still in operation, although without the New Bedford service or name.

Hermogenes "Coochie" Oliveria was a popular purser who meandered through the steamship announcing the upcoming port. When the Nantucket steamship docked on the Vineyard, Coochie would announce, "Oak-a Bluffs, Oak-a Bluffs, Change here for Vinn-Haven, Edgartown and all parts of Marth's Vineyard. This steamer is for Naaaaaaaantucket!"[101]

Captain Charles Leighton (1896–1950) epitomized the role of a Vineyard steamship captain. In 1924, he was first named in command of the steamer *Pequot*, which ferried passengers between Woods Hole and the Vineyard.

John Leighton, Charles's father, served as a steward on the steamer *Monohansett* and was listed as master mariner in 1896. Young Charles began his steamship career in 1912 as dishwasher and waiter aboard ship at the age of sixteen. The teenager did his job well and performed several positions as he matured up the ranks, from baggage man to quartermaster to pilot and eventually captain.

In 1918, Charles Leighton married Florence Jackson of Nantucket, daughter of Levi Jackson. (Jackson conducted the dramatic rescue of the crew of the *Mertie B. Crowley* off Chappaquiddick in 1910.) At the time, Leighton was pilot of the *Uncatena*, and after his wedding, in Nantucket, he flew flags from his masthead and blew the ship's whistle three times for his bride.

At twenty-four, Leighton earned his master's license then worked as pilot of the *Sankaty* and the *Myles Standish* under Captain Francis Marshall and then Captain Manuel Sylvia.

In August 1924, Captain Sylvia was injured while at the helm of the *Pequot*, prompting Leighton to be promoted to captain. Charles Leighton was twenty-eight, the youngest steamship captain aboard a Vineyard boat.

Later that year, Leighton graduated from Northeastern with a degree in law. It was duly noted that Charles Leighton had never graduated from high school yet successfully completed his college curriculum. Captain Leighton enjoyed music and directed the minstrels of 1925 in a benefit for the Martha's Vineyard Hospital. He supported the local basketball team and served on the school committee for years.

In 1934, Leighton was named captain of the *Martha's Vineyard* when Captain Manuel Sylvia retired. Not only did Leighton succeed Sylvia on the high seas, he also bought Sylvia's house on Main Street in Edgartown, moving his wife and four children from their home adjacent to the *Vineyard Gazette*.

In 1936, an eleven-year-old stowaway was discovered aboard the *Nantucket*. The New Bedford preteen wanted to get to the Vineyard to see the movie star Jimmy Cagney. Captain Leighton ensured that the boy was fed but returned him to New Bedford without meeting Cagney.

On July 2, 1940, the *Gazette* reported that while at the helm of the *New Bedford*, Captain Leighton rescued eight people aboard a sailboat in flames off Oak Bluffs. Leighton had the boat towed in and the passengers taken to the hospital.

The Leightons' two sons, Charles Jr. (Chuck) and Samuel (Bud), both served in the marines during the war.

In 1945, Captain Leighton directed a rescue operation to save four people whose sailboat had capsized off Squash Meadow Oak Bluffs. Leighton was in the *Nantucket* and ordered a lifeboat launched to save them. "The rescue by the steamboat was effected so expeditiously, despite the difficulties, that only twenty minutes of running time was lost."[102]

After two days without steamship service in 1945, due to a devastating pre-winter storm, a steamship eventually arrived on the Vineyard, with Captain Leighton at the helm: "It is doubtful if an arriving steamer has been as welcome in many a generation."[103]

Another reliable, respected captain was James Sandsbury. "A gentleman of erect posture and meticulous appearance, he possessed the poise and carriage appropriate to a ship's master. His resonant voice and bespectacled, mustached face were familiar to everyone who traveled on the line."[104]

When state management took over in 1949, Captain Sandsbury retired. He had served as captain of the *Gay Head*, *Uncatena*, *Sankaty*, *Martha's Vineyard*, *Nantucket*, *New Bedford* and *Naushon*. He began under the old side-wheeler *Nantucket* in 1909 and retired when the *Islander* was about to be introduced. With Captain Sandsbury's retirement, Captain Leighton became the senior captain of the Island fleet.

At the end of March 1950, Captain Charles Leighton died of a heart attack shortly after he docked the *Martha's Vineyard* at the New Bedford wharf. "People found it hard to believe that the familiar and friendly figure of Charlie Leighton—as almost everyone knew him—would not be seen again on the bridge of an Island steamer."[105]

The Edgartown school and local businesses were closed for Leighton's funeral. Flags flew at half-staff. Captain Charles Leighton was fifty-four.

Charles Leighton has descendants on Island. His grandson Charlie is in the Bodes, an Edgartown band formed in the 1960s. Great-granddaughter Erin lives and works in Edgartown, and great-great-grandson Charlie was born on January 25, 2018.

Chapter 13

BUSES, TRUCKS AND TOUR BUSES

1920–PRESENT

The taxi is one of the more utilitarian vehicles in urban areas. In the 1920s on the Vineyard, taxis succeeded the original jitney. Jim Norton's grandfather was the first to operate taxis on Martha's Vineyard, establishing headquarters on Main Street in Vineyard Haven, at the site of the former Bowl and Board. The grandson of whaleman Ellsworth West founded Stagecoach Taxi in honor of his grandfather. Adam Wilson started Adam's Cab and went on to serve in town governments. Today's taxi vans accommodate myriad tourists who arrive on the Vineyard in need of a ride.

"Among the motor vehicles on the Island was an open-sided bus owned by the Sibley brothers in Edgartown. It carried arriving vacationers from the ferries to the hotels. As the roads improved, it was also used for sightseeing trips up-Island."[106] Sibley's Garage of Edgartown served Edgartown, Oak Bluffs, Vineyard Haven and Gay Head.

Once trolley service concluded, jitneys ran the roads. "For a brief period afterward, jitneys—unregulated, owner-operated automobile taxis which were successfully outcompeting streetcars nationwide—filled travelers' needs."[107]

The jitney was replaced by scheduled bus service organized by a local entrepreneur. "Harry Horton's bus line was the principal service for down-Island summertime commuters." Horton had two big, bulky Reo buses. He picked up passengers at the old trolley waiting room in Oak Bluffs and dropped them at Tilton's Drug Store, in Vineyard Haven. (Later this was the site of Yates' Drugstore, now Claudia's Jewelry Store.) "Horton's buses left

Horton's bus service transported passengers between Oak Bluffs and Vineyard Haven. *Courtesy of Martha's Vineyard Antique Photos.*

for Oak Bluffs on the hour. I believe he had about two of them, so he gave pretty good service," recalled Stan Lair. Horton drove his bus out to Gay Head for school field trips. Harry Horton's buses operated for a number of years from late spring through the summer, capturing both the local and tourist crowds.

Horton's Bus Line placed ads as early as the summer of 1922. John Canha recalled the thrill of the bus ride between Oak Bluffs and Vineyard Haven. He also had fond memories of the trip with his school class out to Gay Head on the bus. About the same time, in 1923, the Scoville brothers operated sightseeing buses, known as Vineyard Line Tours, out of Vineyard Haven.

Horton's bus service survived into the 1930s. It may have served the needs of the patrons of Reverend Oscar Denniston. Participants in his Bradley Memorial Church met at Noepe Hall by the present Strand Theater in Oak Bluffs. Congregants from across the Island arrived by the busload each summer Sunday.

Sightseeing buses were introduced on the Vineyard after World War II. An early advertisement from 1947 to promote the tour bus service noted that it provided a guided tour of the Vineyard with highlights still worth seeing three-quarters of a century later.

"My dad was a very jovial person," recalled Jules BenDavid. "He had the bus company with open-air buses. I was in the garage business and went back to work for my dad." Arthur BenDavid started Martha's Vineyard Sightseeing in the 1940s with open-air buses similar to those run by Henry Horton. Each bus had twenty seats in rows, with open sides and a canopy roof. The route they followed was similar to the tour buses of the twenty-first century, venturing up and around the Island, covering approximately fifty-five miles

The jitney, or omnibus, would go where the trolley could not and was cheaper. This led to the demise of the trolley system. *Courtesy of the Connie Sanborn collection.*

in two and a half hours. Jules BenDavid took over the company in 1978 and ran it until 1990.

Another tour bus company, Gay Head Sightseeing, was run by Kenny Rose and later purchased by the owner of the *Island Queen*. Jules BenDavid was working for the *Island Queen*, which ran a shuttle between Oak Bluffs and Edgartown. BenDavid was hired by the *Island Queen* to run both bus companies. "I had fifty people working for me and thirty buses," he recalled. He incorporated the two companies with identifiable colors—Martha's Vineyard Sightseeing (blue) and Gay Head Sightseeing (white and purple)—under two licenses. His original buses were school buses.

"I was pretty active in my younger years," says Jules with a smile.

The company had a repair shop with two mechanics on School Street in the old Whiting Milk Company building. He hired a manager and office staff and owned two buildings on Dockside in Oak Bluffs: the Parasee Building, now the Sand Bar, and the Pit Stop, now the Big Dipper. Wife Barbara worked with him.

To determine the route of the tour bus, BenDavid got permission to drive through the various Island towns and applied for approval from the Department of Public Utilities. "We always went to Menemsha until it got too congested." He recalled it was difficult to turn at the corner of North Water and Winter Streets because tour buses have a long turning radius; the route was curtailed to Church Street in Edgartown. (Today, the corner of North Water and Winter Streets includes an angle to help large vehicles negotiate the turn.)

BenDavid occasionally rode "blind" on one of his tour buses to hear what the drivers said on their route. He had a lot of different drivers over the years. "We had a good crew."

"My sightseeing buses connected with the *Island Queen*, and we took the passengers on tour," said BenDavid. "I managed both companies from the same building." He supplemented his company by adding a couple of gas-powered trolleys. "I sent two men down to Key West to drive them up." That must have been a sight for people on the road. Trolleys proved very popular, just as they were a century earlier.

To further attract attention, "I took a regular bus and cut off the top so it was an open bus. I licensed it with public utilities. I put in roll bars and built it right in my shop. It had a surrey top."

"When the open bus was parked next to the closed one, no one got on the closed bus." Jules BenDavid cut the roof off his shuttle bus to delight tourists. *Courtesy of Barbara BenDavid.*

"I was involved in bringing the *Queen Elizabeth II* to Martha's Vineyard," adds Jules BenDavid. The first cruise ship was the *Britanis* in 1985, but the *QE II* came several times after that. "I became the *QE II* port agent and coordinated with the Coast Guard to bring the *QE II* into Vineyard waters. They needed a port agent at each port. I worked with customs and immigration." The *QEII* had 1,900 passengers and a crew of 1,015; it stood thirteen stories high. BenDavid ran forty-eight tours off the *QE II* on one of its visits. "I enjoy being with people," he says.

Since the 1990s, cruise ships have anchored off Oak Bluffs over the years.

Motor coaches rode over on the steamship for a while, were banned yet now have returned. These leviathans appropriate large sections of the narrow Vineyard roadways. Small fourteen-passenger vans are popular as they are more personal and use less roadway.

When Jules BenDavid retired, it was hard for him not to drive downtown and check on the business—hard to let go.

Martha's Vineyard Sightseeing was sold to Jack Dario in 1990 and continues today with Island-wide tour buses through the summer and well into the autumn. Scott Dario, Jack's son, has operated the company for years. He offers trolley service, wedding transport and a small van under the name of Island Transport.

Since 2012, Susan Bennett has operated Martha's Vineyard Tours and Sightseeing with van service across the Vineyard, meeting the needs of both tourists and locals. Her company offers sightseeing tours and transport vans for weddings and other functions.

School bus service expanded in the mid-twentieth century with the increase in population and the closure of one-room schoolhouses. Regionalization of the high school in 1959 cemented the school bus as a fixture on Island roadways. The bright yellow behemoths dominate morning and afternoon roadways crisscrossing the Island.

The Vineyard Transit Authority (VTA) came into existence in 1980 in response to the needs of locals and tourists. Over the past four decades, as the Vineyard population has grown to eighteen thousand people and the number of tourists has mushroomed, the VTA has proved itself a reliable service to meet the varied needs of the Vineyard. The VTA is the best way to get around the Island without a car and operates year-round.

Driving on the busy Vineyard roads can be difficult. Darren Morris is general manager of Transit Connection, Inc., which runs the VTA. "I think the biggest challenge our drivers face is the vast increase in the number of vehicles here in the summer," says Morris. "People park very poorly, oftentimes in the bus parking spots. Corners become harder to negotiate, and we have trouble staying on schedule when we are sitting in traffic." The Steamship Authority reflects that increase in Island traffic as more than fifty thousand automobiles have been transported on or off the Island each July and August over the past several years.

"The roundabout has greatly improved the flow of traffic at that intersection," added Morris. "However, it has exacerbated the traffic situation at the triangle as vehicles going into Edgartown don't get slowed down anywhere along the way anymore. Kind of a Catch-22."

Also, when automobiles exit the steamship lot in Vineyard Haven, it slows down VTA buses. "Interestingly, the airport has become a bottleneck for us in the last couple of years when the bigger jets come in from New York in the summer," noted Darren Morris. Traffic backs up to the airport terminal because of the difficulty to get out onto the West Tisbury–Edgartown Road.

Morris is proud of his crew. "We have an incredibly dedicated, experienced group of drivers who stick it out and drive the buses through some very tough conditions. I can't say enough about what a fantastic bunch of employees we have that work here as bus drivers." The drivers serve hundreds of passengers a day through the heat and traffic of summer. "They are the best!"

Passenger load fluctuates through the year. In July and August, drivers transport nearly a third of a million passengers a month. In the shoulder season of June and September, numbers are about 150,000 passengers per month. During the rest of the year, when buses are filled primarily with locals, the monthly passenger load ranges to 50,000. This reflects more than a 20 percent increase in passengers over the past seven years.

In 2018, the VTA ran a fleet of thirty-three buses and five vans. Off-season, about a dozen buses are on the road, which doubles in the height of summer. "Vans are a little more consistent with an average of three vans on the road every day," says Darren Morris. About thirty-five drivers work in the off-season and nearly ninety drivers cover routes in the summer. It's a busy operation. Vans are used to transport residents to medical appointments and other services.

The VTA depends on a variety of funding sources beyond the passenger fare of $1.25 per person per town. It is funded by local assessments assigned by the state, charged against individual town tax revenue. "Local assessments are somewhat service based," says Angie Grant of the VTA. Revenue also comes from the Farebox, federal, state and other sources. "We receive federal funding as a reimbursement to expenses from the prior year. So we borrow money to have cash to operate annually," she adds.

The Vineyard Transit Authority is the premier year-round transit service for the Island. It has proven popular with patrons. Service is affordable and efficient. Bus drivers pick up patrons anywhere along their route and now have installed benches for customer comfort at the usual stops. Bus parking areas ease traffic flow and provide safe conditions. Buses accommodate bicycles as well.

The VTA transports automobile drivers to their cars in the Vineyard Haven Park and Ride program to meet the steamships. The VTA has admirably filled a transport vacuum in the needs of the Island for both the tourist in the height of summer and the working person year-round.

"He owns five buildings, including climate-controlled storage facilities, fifty moving vans, trucks and school buses." For more than half a century, Clarence A. "Trip" Barnes III has been moving and storing the personal possessions of the people of Martha's Vineyard.

Barnes got his driver's license at fourteen. Five years later, he bought his first truck, a 1948 Ford, and began work at Carroll's Trucking. "It was really Leigh [Carroll] who taught me my trade," he says. Since that initial foray, Trip Barnes's lifetime career has consisted of packing up personal belongings and furnishings and transporting them on, off or across the Island.[108]

Following stints as a tour bus driver, milkman and trucking groceries from off-Island to Cronig's Market, Barnes and his eponymous Moving and Storage Company have been a fixture on Martha's Vineyard. Barnes has moved pianos, an off-Island ice arena, baskets of cats and even a house from one part of the Vineyard to another.

Now in his late seventies, Barnes revels in memories of his youthful exploits. It's been a good run, and Barnes supplants his résumé with auctioneering opportunities to benefit local charities.

Chapter 14

STEAMSHIP TRAVEL

1950–PRESENT

T he story of the island steamers has been a narrative of constant evolution in the development of navigation under power. Just as steam succeeded sail, and in its turn was displaced by diesel power, so did wood construction give way to steel, and wood fuel lost out to coal, which in turn was succeeded by oil."[109]

The *Islander* (1950–2007) was a double-ended ferry built by the Maryland Dry Dock Company in 1950. It went into service as the first diesel ferry built specifically for the Islands. An actual ferry, like the *Islander*, must be double-ended, meaning it can dock from either end without the need to turn around. Being a double-ender created the "drive-through" effect—no turning around or backing off. The *Islander* was also the first steamship to accommodate large trailer trucks, which signaled a major change in how goods were delivered to the Vineyard.

The *Islander* was 201 feet long; held 48 cars and 771 passengers; and chugged along at more than twelve knots between Woods Hole and Vineyard Haven. It had space for five semi-rigs.

Storms have always been a challenge to steamship service. Not only could trips be cancelled but sometimes boats themselves faced danger. The *Islander* was no exception. On August 31, 1954, Hurricane Carol ravaged New England. The *Islander* was moored in Woods Hole. "Her captain, Alec Smith, thought she might get smashed to bits so he took her over to Lambert's Cove to give her shelter, running her engines slowly ahead to maintain steerage."[110] That decision probably saved the *Islander* from storm damage.

After more than a half century of reliable service, the *Islander* faced retirement. "As the longest-serving boat in Vineyard history, the *Islander* achieved an illusion of permanence that caused its retirement in March 2007 to be particularly wrenching."[111] The steamship was sold to the Governor's Island Preservation and Education Corporation of New York in 2007. It was there only a short time; repairs were not made, and the *Islander* was scrapped at the New Jersey Salvage Shipyard in 2012.

A new vessel, the *Nantucket* (1957–88), was built in the era of diesel engines. The vessel was 229 feet long with a four-thousand-horsepower engine and steamed along at fifteen knots. The ship was awkward both in loading automobiles and in design but plied the Vineyard waters reliably for thirty years. As some critics pointed out, "With bulky lines, electrically operated auxiliary equipment and a stern door suggestive of that found on a packer garbage truck, she was not, to them, a steamer in the traditional sense."[112] It took a while for a new vessel to be accepted, especially by old-timers.

It became evident right away that this new ship did not function well as a ferry. In response to complaints, the front door was welded shut, requiring trucks be backed off, a time-consuming inconvenience. The new *Nantucket*'s short smokestack spread cinders on passengers on the outside deck, which had to be remedied. The steering had to be corrected. Additional crew were employed to meet customer complaints. Most issues were addressed, and passengers learned to appreciate the restrooms, snack bar, added passenger space on deck and smooth ride.

An anomaly at the time of the launch of the new *Nantucket* in 1957 was that the old *Nantucket* had recently undergone a major refurbishment and was still in service.

The *Nobska*, built in 1925, the second ship in the White Fleet, had been renamed the *Nantucket* in 1928. It was refitted to accommodate more automobiles in 1951, and its engine made more efficient. In 1957, it reverted to its original name, the *Nobska*. That made way for the new vessel to be named the *Nantucket*. Eventually, the *Nobska/Nantucket/Nobska* was taken out of service in 1973. "Longevity had made her not just a dowager, but an antique and a symbol of an era gone by, and as such, she paid her way as a popular passenger vessel."[113]

In 1974, the Friends of *Nobska* managed to induce the National Register of Historic Places to induct the *Nobska* into its premier register. The Friends anticipated a noble retirement for their prized vessel. And for a brief time, the *Nobska* served as a floating restaurant in Baltimore. The Friends purchased the *Nobska* in 1988. However, without sufficient funds, the ship languished for nearly two decades in Charlestown Navy Yard until being unceremoniously scrapped in 2006.

Friends of *Nobska* morphed into the New England Steamship Foundation in 1994, intent on creating a steamship museum. Finally, the organization fell apart, mired in controversy, faulty fundraising and bankruptcy.

The *Nobska* and its sister ships represented an integral era in the history of water transport to Martha's Vineyard. With the demise of the *Nobska*, this period of history lost an important representative.

A labor disruption occurred in the spring of 1951 that tied up steamship traffic for two weeks. Mail was delivered by plane to the islands. Fishing vessels and private boats transported freight and passengers to and from the Vineyard.

A more intense labor dispute occurred in the spring of 1960 that gave rise to a strike when the size of the crew on the New Bedford run was reduced. The dispute lingered throughout the spring while Vineyarders expressed anxiety over the anticipated impact on the impending summer season. Small private and fishing boats were once again put into service to haul freight to the island. The strike was not resolved until July 2, lasting seventy-seven days without steamship service to the Vineyard.

The result of the strike was that New Bedford was eliminated as a port by the Steamship Authority. The authority had been established in 1949 specifically to provide service to the Vineyard and Nantucket from the mainland. Woods Hole was a closer terminus than New Bedford; now it became the sole point of departure. The Steamship Authority was renamed the Woods Hole, Martha's Vineyard and Nantucket Steamship Authority and remains under that name today. Responsibility for costs was allocated at 50 percent to the Vineyard, 40 percent to Nantucket and 10 percent to Falmouth (Woods Hole).

Both Islanders and residents of New Bedford were disheartened by this event, caused by the economic limitations of steamship service. It made 1960 a pivotal year in steamship service.

A fire of undetermined origin occurred in midsummer 1965 at the Oak Bluffs wharf. Rebuilding the pier was undertaken, but the Steamship Authority determined it was economically feasible to shift year-round freight transport and commercial goods to the Vineyard Haven pier.

Hyannis became the port for all vessels to and from Nantucket in 1984.

Today, summer passenger service operates between Martha's Vineyard and Nantucket on the Hy-Line ferry system.

Passenger service directly between Falmouth Harbor and Martha's Vineyard began in the 1960s. The Island Commuter Corporation was organized in 1961 with the *Vineyard Queen*, renamed the *Island Queen* in 1965, and replaced by a second *Island Queen* in 1974. Service has continued for half a century. It is faster but slightly more expensive to cross Vineyard Sound on the *Queen* than on the Steamship Authority ferries, and it docks in Dockside in Oak Bluffs and Falmouth Harbor rather than Woods Hole.

The *Uncatena* (1965–93) was built in Warren, Rhode Island, for the Steamship Authority. It had two 750-horsepower diesel engines and was "equipped with a propeller set in an opening at the bow. This device is known as a bow-thruster and permits deft maneuvering for the purpose of docking."[114] This improved the approach to a pier, which reduced pressure on the crew who were only using lines.

The initial reaction to the *Uncatena* was that it was inadequate for the service: too short and unseaworthy. The steamship was made longer so it could accommodate more vehicles; this effort made it more seaworthy. The *Uncatena* was literally severed in half in 1971 and an additional 52.5 feet added to its middle, bringing its overall length to 201.5 feet. The additional length provided more space for the crew and made the boat better adapted to handling rough weather.

With the additional length, the *Uncatena* accommodated fifty-seven cars and three hundred passengers. Extending the length of the steamship was not a secret. Passengers nicknamed the vessel the "Junkatena" or the "Tin can tena." However, when the *Uncatena* was taken out of service in 1993, it was sorely missed when sold down south. Its new name was the *Entertainer*, a gambling vessel for Casino Miami Cruises, later relocated to Tampa, where it was scrapped after being ravaged by Hurricane Ivan in 2004.

Another new vessel, another *Nantucket* (1974–   ), was launched by the Steamship Authority. This vessel is 230 feet long and carries sixty cars and one thousand passengers. "She made her first trip to Martha's Vineyard [in 1974], tying up at Oak Bluffs for island inspection. Stephen Carey Luce made it a point to be on board for that trip, for it was his twelfth maiden crossing on an island steamer."[115]

Passenger compartments are separated by a section on port and starboard. "Each of these side compartments was divided into two sections; the forward section being supplied with comfortable fixed seats and tables, and the after, larger section having large seats, arranged bus style."[116] The *Nantucket* has been a quiet workhorse, in service for forty-five years plying Vineyard Sound.

The old *Nantucket*, built in 1957, was renamed the *Naushon* in 1974 to make way for the new *Nantucket*. When the old *Nantucket/Naushon* was taken out of service, it was the last steamship in service in the United States. When author/historian Tom Dunlop witnessed the final scheduled run of the *Naushon* in 1988, he observed, "The *Naushon* would mark not just the last time a true steamship carried passengers and cars across the waters of Vineyard and Nantucket Sounds, but actually from anywhere to anywhere along the whole Eastern Seaboard of the United States."[117]

The *Naushon* was removed from service in 1988 and converted to a gambling site in Mobile, Alabama. "As is often the case with schemes like this, it did not last. She ended up in a landlocked pond in Mississippi, and after a record flood of the Mississippi River, she was left sitting on the bottom, listing to starboard. She was scrapped in 2012."[118] Once again, a steamship met an ignoble demise.

The *Governor* (1954–   ) was built in 1954 in Oakland, California. Its original name was *Crown City*. In 1970, the double-ender, a true ferry, was sold to the State of Washington and renamed *Kulshan*. The Coast Guard purchased the vessel in 1982 and brought it through the Panama Canal to Governor's Island, New York. The Steamship Authority purchased the *Governor* in 1998 as a supplemental ship. The wide-open decked *Governor* holds fifty-nine cars and 350 passengers. Its diesel electric engine has four thousand horsepower and chugs along at thirteen to fifteen knots.

The speed of steamboats crossing Vineyard Sound has not increased much over the years. When the *Martha's Vineyard*, a side-wheeler, first ventured across the Sound in 1871, it reached a top speed of fifteen knots, comparable to today's vessels. The maximum speed of a ship moving through the water has limits due to water pressure against the hull, the tides, current and ocean swells.

Other steamships in service include the *Martha's Vineyard* (1993), the *Island Home* (2007) and the *Woods Hole* (2016), all sturdy, reliable vessels. Also, three freight boats date back to a previous generation: the *Katama* (1988), the *Gay Head* (1989) and the *Sankaty* (1994). Details on various current steamships are available at www.steamshipauthority.com/about/vessels.

The Steamship Authority maintains its vessels by Coast Guard standards of seaworthy safety. Lifesaving drills are part of the routine. Passenger safety and comfort are always in mind. The people of Martha's Vineyard are fortunate to have a safe and reliable service to count on throughout the year.

Bridget Tobin supervises Steamship Authority freight traffic on the Vineyard. She recalls that in the 1970s and '80s, boats to both Nantucket and the Vineyard left from Woods Hole. Passengers purchased paper tickets. Those headed to the Vineyard were given a green ticket; those headed to Nantucket got a pink slip. Service to Nantucket changed from Woods Hole to Hyannis in 1984. Bridget Tobin retired in 2018 and is sorely missed; she was well known and respected by Islanders.

The Hy-Line links Hyannis to Nantucket but cannot accommodate vehicles. And no vehicles travel between Woods Hole and Nantucket except in unique situations, like an ice storm when trailer trucks transport food to the Gray Lady.

Finding Old Steamship Piers

Finding old cart roads or railroads is easier than locating old steamship wharves. We have to resort to the historical record rather than scrabbling through the fields and woods to uncover evidence of wharves or piers from long ago.

Currently, two towns have piers that accommodate Steamship Authority boats: Vineyard Haven and Oak Bluffs. These wharves have been in use since the first steamships linked the Vineyard with the mainland in the mid-nineteenth century. At least seven additional sites are known where steamships docked through the years:

1. Edgartown was a primary port in the initial stage of steamship service between Nantucket and New Bedford. The Edgartown port was phased out for financial reasons in 1934. Now, a summer vessel has scheduled service between the Observation Wharf in Edgartown Harbor and Falmouth, in summers only. This boat offers valet parking in Falmouth, and passengers reserve seats.

2. South Beach was the site of a pier built in 1873 for the Mattakeset Lodge. Steamships docked there, but it was an arduous trek to deliver tourists from New Bedford or even Woods Hole around the Vineyard to dock at South Beach.

Businessmen supported by Edgartown voters authorized the Martha's Vineyard Railroad to run from Oak Bluffs to Katama. Once the railroad went out of business, the pier was broken down and removed to Chappaquiddick for use in its pavilion.

3. Steamers ran excursions to Gay Head in the late 1800s. Tourists flocked to Oak Bluffs and boarded a steamer for a day in Gay Head. At times, the vessel had a brass band on board. These ventures garnered tourist dollars and benefited Native Americans, who sold pottery and knickknacks. With the success of excursions, restaurants and a hotel were established in Gay Head. Boats docked at the Lighthouse Landing just north of the Gay Head Light.

4. Lambert's Cove had a wharf for boats heading to and from the mainland in the late 1700s. Packets would dock there to transfer passengers or freight. In the late 1800s, there was talk of a landing for boats from New York and excursion steamships from Oak Bluffs docked there. Clay was mined from the hills of Makonikey to be shipped off-Island. The Makonikey Hotel was a short-lived effort to promote tourism in Lambert's Cove in the late 1890s but never succeeded.

5. "The West Chop wharf was made a regular landing of the steamboat line, two hotels were built, a bowling alley, a billiard hall and tennis courts."[119] This was the site of West Point Grove, a land development scheme of the late 1800s. "Through the woods a white shell road was built to Vineyard Haven. The success of West Chop from that time was never in doubt." However, the pier at West Chop never proved as prominent as that of Vineyard Haven or Oak Bluffs.

6. Eastville pier was built in the 1870s for a ferry from New York. (Hence the name New York Avenue.) Remnants can be seen where East Chop Drive turns in from the shore. Horse-drawn trolleys, later electrified, brought

passengers from the pier the mile or so downtown to the Camp Meeting Association. The dock was expanded in the 1890s to meet the desires of the New York Yacht Club.

7. Highland Wharf in Oak Bluffs was built in 1872 by the Vineyard Grove Company for patrons of the Camp Meeting Association. The site allowed revivalists to disembark without being subjected to the amusement park atmosphere of Oak Bluffs. The Highland Wharf was convenient for patrons of the Baptist Tabernacle in the Highlands and the Summer Institute, a popular summer school for teachers along East Chop Drive in the late 1800s.

Today, a number of scheduled vessels run out from Dockside in Oak Bluffs. Tourists flock to the Vineyard from Hyannis and Falmouth on the Cape, New Bedford in southeastern Massachusetts and Quonset, Rhode Island. On occasion, a ferry has operated between Martha's Vineyard and New York.

Chapter 15

GETTING TO THE VINEYARD IN THE TWENTY-FIRST CENTURY

More than a century after Frances Meikelham journeyed from New York to Martha's Vineyard, Olivia Hull of the *Vineyard Gazette* expounded on transportation access routes to Martha's Vineyard in the summer of 2013. "Expanding transportation services among airlines, ferries, buses and trains have made the Vineyard more accessible than ever this summer."[120]

She wrote, "Summer rail service between Boston and the Cape has returned for the first time in 25 years." And added, "The Cape Flyer weekend railway service between Boston and Hyannis was in full swing over the Fourth of July." Railroad service was reinstituted between Boston and Cape Cod, even offering shuttle service from the Buzzards Bay stop to the Steamship Authority in Woods Hole for boats to the Vineyard. However, it is neither fast nor cheap, costing over thirty dollars and taking more than two hours by train.

For Vineyarders without access to an automobile, Peter Pan bus service is the primary means to get to Boston, although it is not cheap; count on at least fifty dollars for a ticket. Barring traffic delays, the bus can reach South Station in an hour and three-quarters, which is comparable to automobile driving. Peter Pan remains the only good ground transportation company connecting carless passengers originating at Woods Hole with Logan Airport. However, there is the White Tie Limousine service for those in the know.

Major airlines, such as Delta and JetBlue, link the Vineyard to New York. And "Cape Air remains the Island's year-round airline with its nine-seat Cessna 402 aircrafts," reported the *Gazette*. "Active management of scheduling allows the airline to be more flexible in terms of meeting demand." Cape Air provides reliable service to Boston.

For more than a half century, the Steamship Authority has proven the most conventional and convenient means of transport to the Vineyard. Even in the depths of winter, Vineyarders can count on more than a dozen trips a day of both passenger and automobile service, year-round, between Woods Hole and Martha's Vineyard.

Since its inception in 1960, the *Island Queen* has maintained a steady summer schedule conveying passengers between Falmouth and Oak Bluffs. It is a mite more expensive yet faster than the steamship. Between Hyannis and Oak Bluffs, the Hy-Line Cruises operate both high-speed and conventional summer service.

The *Island Queen* is dwarfed by the presence of the *Queen Elizabeth II* shortly before the latter ran aground in 1992. *Courtesy of Chris Baer, history.vineyard.net/photos.*

The Martha's Vineyard Fast Ferry operates high-speed summer service between Quonset, Rhode Island, and Oak Bluffs. It has proven popular with the New York, New Jersey and Connecticut market with its convenient connection with Amtrak. The ferry offers business-class amenities for travelers traveling without a car.

The boat from New Bedford, the high-speed passenger ferry *Seastreak*, connects southeastern Massachusetts with Oak Bluffs and also meets the needs of those passengers traveling from New York. Ticketed ferry passengers aboard the *Seastreak* receive a free bus ride between New Bedford and Boston to benefit Islanders.

EPILOGUE

There is a magical draw to Martha's Vineyard. A 1901 guide to the Vineyard promoted the Island's attraction: "The name always attracts attention, and the island is worthy of its name."[121] Martha's Vineyard still resonates, as characterized in a 1965 assessment of the Vineyard by a resident who had seen the Island evolve over the past dozen or so years, with steamships full of cars and new roads and lots of people: "Roofs pop up where only trees grew not long ago. But the island still isn't ruined. In the words of a dour New Englander: 'Not yet.'"[122]

Whether on Martha's Vineyard or "over in America," the only constant in transportation is that it is continually evolving. When the whaleship *Splendid* was towed by a steamship through Vineyard Sound, that represented a change in modes of transportation. When the steam locomotive Active met steamships docked in Oak Bluffs and transported passengers to Katama, the conjunction of two steam-powered modes of transport was in play.

In 1902, when Edward Mulligan was behind the wheel of his horseless carriage and startled an actual horse pulling a wagon in Vineyard Haven, the juxtaposition of old and new means of transport faced off against each other. And when the first airplane splashed into Oak Bluffs Harbor, it created an urge to fly among summer people who sought a faster route to reach their vacation homes.

Change is the only constant. When locals can adapt to a new steamship or a new means of transport, the Island benefits.

Yet not every means of movement succeeds. The moped at first seemed to be a respectable mode of transport for tourists. However, successive accidents, leading to injuries and in some cases death, hindered its acceptance. Additionally, there is no appropriate space for the moped on Vineyard roadways; neither the bicycle paths that stretch across down-Island nor the various roadways have a lane or route for mopeds. The moped rider sinks beneath the radar of safe transportation. The movement to ban the moped is a positive step by serious safety-conscious Vineyarders.

As patrons of a consistently more mobile society, we should not lose sight of our past, our origins, the primitive means by which we traversed the Island for decades, even centuries. Horseback riding, walking and bicycling are all appropriate, enjoyable means to savor the sites of the Vineyard, safely and pollution-free. Bike paths, horse trails and walking trails spread across the state forest and the wilds of the Vineyard. They are there to be sampled, savored and saved. And whether on the back of a horse, on a bicycle seat, behind the wheel of a car or on foot, we depend on reliable, efficient routes to get us to the next leg on our journey.

Who knows what the future holds? "They say" steamships don't move much faster than they did a century ago because friction of water against a boat's hull has a limit. Who knows? That may change. Automobiles can only go so fast—until they are built more efficiently or roadways are widened and leveled out. Bus service is efficient; yet if people don't patronize the bus, will it remain running?

We respect the relics of our past, assume responsibility for the problems of the present and plan for the most optimum possibilities of the future.

NOTES

Chapter 1

1. Foster, *A Meeting of Land and Sea*, 98.
2. Ibid., 80.
3. Ibid., 85.
4. Ibid., 104.

Chapter 2

5. Morris and Morin, *Island Steamers*, 3.
6. Ibid.
7. Turner, *Story of the Island Steamers*, 18.
8. Ibid., 21.
9. Ibid., 23.
10. Hough, *Martha's Vineyard, Summer Resort*, 24.
11. *Vineyard Gazette*, August 1854.
12. Zinn, *People's History*, 16.
13. Morris and Morin, *Island Steamers*, 11.

Chapter 3

14. Urban Survival Site, "How to Make Hardtack: A Cracker that Lasts for Years," urbansurvivalsite.com/make-your-own-hardtack.
15. Ibid.
16. Foster, *A Meeting of Land and Sea*, 170.
17. Notes from Cynthia Aguilar.
18. Tod Dimmick, *Martha's Vineyard Magazine*, September 2007.
19. Foster, *A Meeting of Land and Sea*, 170.
20. Ibid.
21. Martha's Vineyard: A Meeting of Land Sea, "The 1850 Map by Henry Laurens Whiting," mvlandandsea.com/the1850map.
22. E-mail from David Foster, December 4, 2017.
23. Hough, *Martha's Vineyard, Summer Resort*, 23.
24. Dimmick, *Martha's Vineyard Magazine*, September 2007.
25. E-mail from Bow Van Riper, November 13, 2017.
26. Dimmick, *Martha's Vineyard Magazine*, September 2007.
27. Foster, *A Meeting of Land and Sea*, 156.

Chapter 4

28. Hough, *Martha's Vineyard, Summer Resort*, 52.
29. *Tours and Guide to Southern MA*, 27.
30. Gene Baer, *Dukes County Intelligencer*.
31. Ewen, *Steamboats to Martha's Vineyard*, 20.
32. *Vineyard Gazette*, August 23, 1935.
33. *Vineyard Gazette*, July 25, 1892.
34. Morris and Morin, *Island Steamers*, 35.

Chapter 5

35. Karl Zimmerman, *Martha's Vineyard Magazine*, 2015.

Chapter 6

36. Page, *Rails Across Martha's Vineyard*, 54.

37. Gene Baer, *Dukes County Intelligencer*.
38. Page, *Rails Across Martha's Vineyard*, 48.
39. Gene Baer, *Dukes County Intelligencer*.
40. Page, *Rails Across Martha's Vineyard*, 50.
41. Gene Baer, *Dukes County Intelligencer*.
42. Ibid.
43. *Martha's Vineyard Isle of Dreams*, 22.

Chapter 7

44. Steve Vancour, *Dukes County Intelligencer*, November 1993.
45. *Vineyard Gazette*, April 17, 1874.
46 *Vineyard Gazette*, September 3, 2009.
47. Ibid.
48. Tom Dunlop, *Vineyard Gazette*, September 3, 2009.
49. *Vineyard Gazette*, August 28, 1874.
50. Tom Dunlop, *Martha's Vineyard Magazine*, Fall 1991.
51. Ibid.
52. Dunlop, *Vineyard Gazette*, September 3, 2009.
53. Hough, *Martha's Vineyard, Summer Resort*, 122.
54. Page, *Rails Across Martha's Vineyard*, 38.
55. Information confirmed in conversation with Alex Palmer, January 5, 2018.
56. Hough, *Martha's Vineyard, Summer Resort*, 263.

Chapter 8

57. *Dukes County Intelligencer*, November 1979.
58. *Dukes County Intelligencer*, February 1986.
59. Ibid.
60. Huntington, *Introduction to Martha's Vineyard*, 10.
61. Ibid., 11.
62. *Vineyard Gazette*, June 30, 1892.
63. Mayhew, *Martha's Vineyard*, 90.
64. *Vineyard Gazette*, October 23, 2003.
65. Hough, *Martha's Vineyard, Summer Resort*, 26.
66. Ibid., 195.

Chapter 9

67. Chris Baer, *Martha's Vineyard Times*, January 25, 2018.
68. *Vineyard Gazette*, February 20, 1874.
69. Chris Baer, *Martha's Vineyard Times*, January 25, 2018.
70. *Picturesque Martha's Vineyard*.
71. *Vineyard Gazette*, August 9, 1900.
72. *Vineyard Gazette*, September 6, 1900.
73. Joseph Chase Allen, *Vineyard Gazette*, 1957.
74. Ibid.
75. Ibid.
76. Ibid.
77. Railton, *The History of Martha's Vineyard*, 341.
78. Ibid., 332.

Chapter 10

79. Zimmerman, *Martha's Vineyard Magazine*, August 1, 2010.
80. *Vineyard Gazette*, August 30, 1900.
81. *Lifeline to the Islands*, 18.
82. Morris and Morin, *Island Steamers*, 51.
83. Ibid., 64.
84. *Vineyard Gazette*, October 25, 1923; reprinted October 20, 2017, *Gazette Chronicle*, comp. by Hilary Wall.

Chapter 11

85. *Boston Post*, July 22, 1919.
86. *Vineyard Gazette*, July 31, 1919.
87. *Dukes County Intelligencer*, August 1993.
88. *Vineyard Gazette*, August 21, 1900.
89. *Vineyard Gazette*, July 16, 1929.
90. Vineyard Conservation Society, "The MV Tap Map," www.vineyardconservation.org/httpssitesgooglecomavineyardconservationorg vineyard-conservation-societyHome.

Chapter 12

91. Ewen, *Steamboats to Martha's Vineyard*, 61.
92. Morris and Morin, *Island Steamers*, 73.
93. Ibid.
94. Ewen, *Steamboats to Martha's Vineyard*, 49.
95. Morris and Morin, *Island Steamers*, 90.
96. Ibid., 85.
97. *Vineyard Gazette*, May 25, 1928.
98. Conversation with Herb Ward, chronicler of the Levi Jackson family history.
99. Telephone conversation with Jimmy Morgan.
100. Morris and Morin, *Island Steamers*, 113.
101. Ibid., 123.
102. *Vineyard Gazette*, August 24, 1945.
103. *Vineyard Gazette*, December 7, 1945.
104. Morris and Morin, *Island Steamers*, 128.
105. *Vineyard Gazette*, March 31, 1950.

Chapter 13

106. Railton, *The History of Martha's Vineyard*, 340.
107. Chris Baer, *Martha's Vineyard Times*, December 14, 2017.
108. Phyllis Meras, *Martha's Vineyard Magazine*, Winter–Spring 2017–18.

Chapter 14

109. Morris and Morin, *Island Steamers*, 177.
110. Healy, *Martha's Vineyard Ferries*, 16.
111. Zimmerman, *Martha's Vineyard Magazine*, August 1, 2010.
112. Morris and Morin, *Island Steamers*, 137.
113. Ibid., 160.
114. *Lifeline to the Islands*, 77.
115. Morris and Morin, *Island Steamers*, 164.
116. Ibid., 165.
117. Ewen, *Steamboats to Martha's Vineyard*, 6.
118. Ibid., 122.
119. Hough, *Martha's Vineyard, Summer Resort*, 232.

Chapter 15

120. Olivia Hull, *Vineyard Gazette*, July 11, 2013.

Epilogue

121. *Pocket Directory Guide*, 9.
122. Shirley Ann Grace, *New York Times Magazine*, August 15, 1965.

BIBLIOGRAPHY

Blackwell, Walter. *Finding the Route of the Martha's Vineyard Railroad, 1874–1896*. Miami: Englelhard Printing Co., 1971.

Ewen, William. *Steamboats to Martha's Vineyard and Nantucket*. Charleston, SC: Arcadia Publishing, 2015.

Foster, David. *A Meeting of Land and Sea*. New Haven, CT: Yale University Press, 2017.

Healy, Everett. *Martha's Vineyard Ferries*. Tisbury, MA: Tisbury Printer, 2015.

Hough, Henry Beetle. *Martha's Vineyard, Summer Resort, 1835–1935*. Rutland VT: Academy Books, 1936.

Huntington, Gale. *An Introduction to Martha's Vineyard*. Oak Bluffs, MA: DaRosa Corporation, 1969.

Mayhew, Eleanor Ransom. *Martha's Vineyard: A Short History and Guide*. Edgartown, MA: Dukes County Historical Society, 1956.

Morris, Paul, and Joseph Morin. *The Island Steamers*. Nantucket, MA: Nantucket Nautical Publishers, 1977.

Page, Herman. *Rails Across Martha's Vineyard: Steam Narrow Gauge and Trolley Lines*. Newton, KS: Mennonite Press, 2009.

Railton, Arthur. *The History of Martha's Vineyard*. Beverly, MA: Commonwealth Editions (in association with the Martha's Vineyard Historical Society), 2006.

Simon, Anne. *No Island Is an Island: The Ordeal of Martha's Vineyard*. Garden City, NY: Doubleday & Company, 1973.

Turner, Henry. *The Story of the Island Steamers*. Nantucket, MA: Inquirer and Mirror Press, 1910.

Whitman, Herbert. *Exploring Old Martha's Vineyard*. Old Greenwich, CT: Chatham Press, 1985.

Zinn, Howard. *A People's History of the United States*. New York: HarperCollins, 1980; repr. 2003.

Guidebooks

Lifeline to the Islands. Woods Hole, Martha's Vineyard and Nantucket Steamship Authority, 1977.

Martha's Vineyard: The Isle of Dreams and Health. Oak Bluffs, MA: Vineyard Publishing Company, 1932.

Picturesque Martha's Vineyard. New York: George Richardson & Co., 1909.

Pocket Directory Guide. January 1901.

Tours and Guide to Southern MA: Campground, Oak Bluffs, Vineyard Highlands and Falmouth Heights. 1868.

Periodicals

Boston Post
Dukes County Intelligencer
Martha's Vineyard Magazine
Martha's Vineyard Times
Massachusetts Historical Commission
New York Times
Vineyard Gazette

INDEX

A

Active 69, 70, 74, 76, 77, 79, 147
airplane 111, 147

C

catboat 88
Charles W. Morgan 108
Civil War 26, 27, 30, 39, 41
Cottage City Street Railway 58

D

Dr. Fisher Road 31, 34, 35, 36, 37, 38

E

Eastville 41, 46, 48, 50, 53, 54, 141
electric trolley car 60

G

Gay Head 16, 25, 38, 42, 44, 45, 50,
        56, 60, 88, 95, 106, 125, 127,
        128, 141
Grant, Ulysses S. 42

H

Highland Wharf 43, 47, 48, 49, 142
horse-drawn trolley 48, 53
Horton's Bus Line 128
hydroplane 110

K

Katama Airfield 111, 112, 113, 114
Katama Land and Wharf Company
        64, 65

L

Lambert's Cove 19, 50, 57, 135, 141

M

Martha's Vineyard Railroad 63, 65,
        67, 68, 70, 73, 74, 76, 77, 78,
        79, 85, 141
Mattakeset Lodge 64, 65, 74, 85, 141

O

Oak Bluffs Land and Wharf Company
        42, 47, 64, 65

Old Colony Railroad 41, 42, 44, 47,
     63, 70, 76
oxen 16

P

packets 19

R

roadways 94

S

seamen's bethel 91

V

Vineyard Grove Company 47, 142

W

Wampanoag 15
Wesleyan Grove 39, 40, 47, 48
White Fleet 115
World War I 60, 109
World War II 122